Angling Books: A Collector's Guide

Angling Books

A Collector's Guide

KEITH HARWOOD

COCH-Y-BONDDU BOOKS
ANGLING MONOGRAPHS SERIES NO. 3
2016

ANGLING BOOKS: A COLLECTOR'S GUIDE
TWO HUNDRED AND FIFTY NUMBERED PAPERBOUND COPIES
PLUS TWENTY-SIX LETTERED HARDBOUND COPIES
HAVE BEEN PRODUCED IN THE
COCH-Y-BONDDU BOOKS ANGLING MONOGRAPHS SERIES

THIS COPY IS NUMBER ....

© Coch-y-Bonddu Books Ltd 2016
Text © Keith Harwood

ISBN 978 1 904784 70 8

Coch-y-Bonddu Books Ltd
Machynlleth, Powys, SY20 8DG
01654 702837
www.anglebooks.com

Contents

For my grandchildren

Acknowledgements

A number of people have provided assistance in the preparation of this book. First of all, I would like to thank my publisher, Paul Morgan of Coch-y-Bonddu Books, who suggested that I write this book and gave me every encouragement. Jon Ward-Allen of Medlar Press and *Waterlog* magazine kindly allowed me to use material that had appeared in that magazine. Angling historian John Austin read through several of the chapters and stopped me from making too many errors.

However, my greatest debt of thanks is to my wife Helen who knows far more about computers than I shall ever know and, on several occasions, magically retrieved material that I had accidentally deleted.

Clitheroe, January 2016

Introduction

In 1955, the National Book League, a forerunner of the current Book Trust, published a little booklet written by Arthur Ransome and bearing the title *Fishing*. The National Book League was established in 1924 by the Society of Bookmen to promote reading and published readers' guides on a number of subjects including: Detective Fiction, Historical Fiction, King and Parliament, Scottish History and the History of Flying. Each booklet contained an annotated bibliography of titles on the subject and Ransome was chosen to write the guide on fishing because of his angling expertise and for his wide-ranging knowledge of angling literature. Ransome's book is still readily available and was re-issued by Cambridge University Press in 2013. In 1995, the Flyfishers' Classic Library produced a new edition of this classic work with a Preface written by Tom Fort and entitled *The Fisherman's Library*. Copies of this edition, too, are still available, and the book is a useful addition to the modern angler's library.

The books listed in Ransome's book formed a solid foundation for building an angler's library and when I started collecting angling books almost forty years ago I found his guide extremely useful in forming my own collection. In 2008, I decided that it would be a good idea to bring Ransome's list of angling books up to date. Many hundreds, if not thousands, of angling books were published between 1995 and 2008, and I persuaded Jon Ward-Allen of *Waterlog* magazine to publish my updated lists. These lists appeared in three parts in the Spring, Summer and Autumn issues of *Waterlog*.

Another seven years have passed since those updated lists were published and many more angling books have appeared on the scene. The world now seems a much smaller place, and books from the United States, and even farther afield, are now much more readily available and give the angling book collector a much wider scope to add to his collection. Paul Morgan of Coch-y-Bonddu Books thought it would be a good idea to update this list yet again to take into account the plethora of angling books published between 1955 and 2015. He also suggested that I write a section on the collecting of angling books and so this book was born. Ransome's list was made up exclusively of British angling books and I have followed suit. To include books published in the USA and elsewhere would have required a book at least twice the length.

The book itself is divided into two parts, the first covering various aspects of collecting angling books and the second, entitled *The Angler's Library*, contains annotated lists of my recommended fishing books. I regard myself as an all-round angler and am just as happy catching a wild brown trout on a fly of my own tying as I am catching a chub on a lump of cheese paste. My angling library, too, reflects my wide ranging interests and is an eclectic mix of book on coarse, game and sea fishing. As a writer and angling historian, I have a particular interest in the long history of our sport and much of my collecting in recent years has been focused on these areas. I do not collect books as an investment, I collect them purely out of interest and I feel this is the best basis for building up a collection of angling books.

The first part of this book is very much based on my own experience of collecting angling books and the books, booklets and magazines featured form part of my angling library. I make no apologies for this since I truly believe that the best books are written from personal experience. My collection of angling books, and the process of collecting them, has given me a great deal of pleasure over the last four decades and I hope the reader, too, will be inspired to start a collection of his/her own.

Part One

THE ANGLING
BOOK COLLECTOR

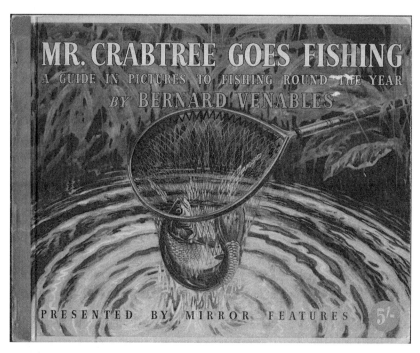

Front and rear covers of the scarce first edition of *Mr. Crabtree Goes Fishing* (1949)

CHAPTER ONE

The Angling Bibliophile

I think it was Arthur Ransome who wrote that some of the best fishing is done in print and I am inclined to agree with him. Throughout my life I have had a fascination for books and I well remember the feeling of excitement when I received my first hardback book complete with dust wrapper as a Christmas present over fifty years ago. If I remember rightly it was one of Enid Blyton's *Famous Five* books and it wasn't long before I had built up a collection of her other books. *Dandy* and *Beano* annuals soon swelled my book collection. As I grew older my reading habits grew more refined and, as I spent most of my adult life teaching Classics and Archaeology, it is not surprising that I built up a large collection of texts on these topics, the majority of which I sold when I retired from teaching. For the last thirty years or so I have been an avid collector of angling books. During that time I have managed to amass a considerable library and collecting angling books is still the main focus of my collecting efforts.

The collecting of angling books is very much akin to angling itself; it brings out the atavistic instinct in me. Coming across a previously unexplored antiquarian bookshop is like coming across a new stretch of water. I simply do not know what it will yield. Nine times out of ten I come away disappointed, with my wallet safely intact. Occasionally, however, I will come across a gem of a book that is a must have for my collection and I exit the shop triumphantly. Such was the case in Thirsk a few years ago when I came across a lovely copy of Dick Walker's *No Need to Lie* (1964), complete with dust wrapper, for a pittance. Nowadays, a good copy of this book complete with dust wrapper is likely to set you back in excess of £200. Such findings, however, are rare and sadly the bookshop in Thirsk has since closed.

During the last thirty years the way in which I buy books has changed considerably. One of my great pleasures involved touring an area of the country equipped with the latest booksellers' guide and visiting the various second-hand and antiquarian bookshops along the way and, back in the 70s and 80s, most small towns had at least one such bookshop. Now, that is no longer the case and over the last decade or so I have been greatly saddened to see the closure of so many bookshops.

Booksellers' catalogues were another prime source of adding to my collection. I take great delight when such a catalogue drops through my letterbox. It is a great pleasure, with a glass of whisky in hand, to browse through the myriad of books on offer and to narrow down the books I want or can afford to buy to one or two. The catalogues themselves are often collectable in their own right and can provide a useful tool for bibliographic reference and prices. Unfortunately, over the last decade the number of catalogues dropping through my letterbox has declined considerably.

My other main sources of acquiring angling books are book and angling fairs, which are held on a regular basis. Every winter I eagerly await the publication of the PBFA's (Provincial Booksellers Fairs Association) calendar of book fairs and I plan my own calendar around them. The highlight of the year is undoubtedly the annual York National Book Fair, held in September, where around two hundred booksellers from around the country and abroad exhibit their wares. Other fairs, which I regularly attend, include Harrogate, Ilkley, Cambridge, Kendal, Clitheroe and Haydock Park. I generally like to arrive early at these fairs before the stalls have been picked over by other collectors and again the anticipation of what I might find is similar to the experience of what I might catch when setting out on a day's fishing. Vintage tackle, game and fly fairs are other good venues for finding that elusive tome to add to my collection and I regularly attend those within a reasonable driving distance.

The main reason for the decline of the bookshop and booksellers' catalogues is the growth of the internet. Many owners of second-hand bookshops simply cannot compete with the lower overheads of internet booksellers and have been forced to close their shops or switch to selling via the internet themselves. The same is true of catalogues; it is much cheaper for booksellers to advertise their wares on-line than to run to the expense of printing and posting out catalogues. On-line catalogues take away much of the pleasure of browsing. I do not like looking at endless pages of lists on a computer screen and would much rather browse through the pages of a printed catalogue while relaxing in an armchair. The internet is also making it more difficult for genuine dealers to acquire second-hand books. According to the owner of my local second-hand bookshop (now closed) many people with books surplus to their requirements are

selling them on eBay in the hope of obtaining a higher price for them rather than taking them to their local bookshop. However, *caveat emptor*, not everything on eBay is as it seems and there are some unscrupulous sellers out there who try to deceive by giving a false or misleading description of a book. I recently came across a copy of the Rev. Houghton's *British Fresh-Water Fishes* for sale on eBay at the buy-it-now price of £200 – a real bargain since the book usually sells for four or five times that price. I very nearly bought that book until I realised it was not a first edition with the coloured plates that was on offer but a second edition with black and white plates, which normally sells for less than fifty pounds. The bookseller's description was deliberately misleading and it could have proved a costly mistake had I bought it. Since I first wrote this I have acquired a first edition of *British Fresh-Water Fishes*, which I came across in a second-hand bookshop in a sleepy little town in Norfolk and I did pay considerably more than £200 for it. It is a lovely copy of that famous work and now takes pride of place on my bookshelves.

The internet is not all bad news and does have some advantages. It makes it much easier to buy books from abroad and I now regularly buy books from the States and am amazed at how quickly they arrive, often more quickly than books ordered from this country. It is also possible, via web-sites such as Abebooks which has access to booksellers world-wide, to track down elusive volumes and to compare the prices of various dealers before making a purchase. On the other hand, booksellers too have access to these prices before pricing their own books and it is now becoming much harder to find a bargain out there. I recently received a catalogue from a bookseller (who shall be nameless) which offered a copy of Ernest Briggs' *Angling and Art in Scotland* (1908) for sale at £285. Shortly afterwards I received another catalogue from a very reputable bookseller listing the same book, in the same edition (there was only one edition), in similar condition for £85. Why the huge difference? It seems to make no sense whatsoever. Another example concerns a more recent book, *An Incompleat Angler* (1976) by Lord Hardinge of Penshurst, which normally sells for around ten pounds, yet one bookseller was listing it at £75. These are but two examples of many more which I could cite. It certainly pays to do your research before purchasing a book.

An **Incompleat Angler**

A Fishing Autobiography

Lord Hardinge of Penshurst

I do not collect angling books as an investment. I buy books because I want to read them or because they are useful for the research I am carrying out. During my thirty years or so as an angling book collector I have seen the value of my angling collection rise and fall. Before the financial crisis of 2008 angling books seemed to be rising steadily in value. Now the bottom seems to have dropped out of the market and some books are selling on the internet for little more than the cost of their postage. I was disappointed when recently I sold off a number of angling books. My wife decided that we needed some new dining room furniture and, as a result, one of my bookcases had to go to make room for the new furniture. I decided to have a sort out of my books and get rid of some that were surplus to my requirements or which I had bought on impulse and now regretted buying. I took the books to a dealer in Yorkshire, one of whose specialities is angling books, and I was very disappointed with what I received for them. After packing them up and taking them over to Yorkshire I could not be bothered to take them to another dealer. If I had had more space I would not have sold them.

Some of my books, however, have risen greatly in value and when they are eventually sold will almost certainly make far more than what I paid for them. When I first started collecting angling books most of the books on coarse fishing could be bought relatively cheaply but, with the growth of specimen hunting and the targeting of single fish species, some prices have risen sharply. Carp anglers or barbel fishers are now eager to devour the literature on their favoured species

THE
Biggest Fish Of All

The Perchfishers

and the limited supply of some books has outstripped demand. Relatively few books have been written on perch, that most ubiquitous of fishes, and those books that have appeared now command high prices. Other books in my library like Oliver Kite's *A Fisherman's Diary* (1969) or Roger Fogg's *The Art of the Wet Fly* (1979) seemed to rise sharply in price soon after going out of print but have since remained relatively stable or even lowered in price.

My angling library covers a broad area from books on coarse, game and sea fishing to volumes on individual fish species and on fly dressing and tackle collecting. During the years I have been collecting my tastes in angling books have changed. When I first started collecting I was mainly a coarse angler with the occasional foray after still-water trout and most of my book purchases were in these areas. Like many other anglers of my generation, the first angling book I ever owned was a copy of *Mr Crabtree Goes Fishing* by Bernard Venables which appeared unexpectedly in my Christmas stocking when I was ten or eleven years old. I was immediately spellbound by the atmospheric cartoons in the book and dreamt of fishing the wonderful venues where Mr Crabtree took Peter. The Hampshire Avon seemed like Nirvana to a youngster brought up on fishing the mill lodges and canals of northern England. Not surprisingly, when I first started collecting angling books seriously, the books of Bernard Venables were at the top of my wants list. In those days his books could be bought relatively cheaply and I am amazed at some of the prices they now command. Other authors whose works I eagerly collected in my early days included Fred J Taylor, Dick Walker, and BB (Denys Watkins-Pitchford). Although I have most of his books, I have never been a massive fan of Dick Walker's writing. Walker was a scientist and engineer who undoubtedly had a tremendous influence on angling in the latter half of the twentieth century. His books contain a mine of useful information, some of which is now dated, but somehow he fails to capture the essence of time spent by the waterside. His best book, as far as I am concerned is *No Need to Lie* (1964), with the wonderful illustration of a hooked carp painted by Reg Cooke on the dust wrapper. By contrast, the works of BB manage to encapsulate

all that is magical about angling – the atmosphere, the scenery, the wildlife and even the fish themselves. BB was an artist as well as a writer and he writes with the eye of an artist, yet with the detail of a supremely knowledgeable naturalist. His books, and my favourite is *Letters from Compton Deverell* (1950), transport us to a world that has now largely vanished, a world where life was lived at a gentler pace and where farmers made hay, not silage. It is a world that I can just remember from my childhood and one for which I feel increasing nostalgia.

Of modern angling writers there are, it seems to me, very few who can match the literary powers of BB. One such writer is Chris Yates, a true angling eccentric who eschews the use of modern tackle in favour of cane rods and centre-pin reels. For him, angling is an activity that is not to be taken too seriously, an activity to be savoured and not rushed, an activity that demands copious amounts of tea brewed from a Kelly

Kettle and the eating of much fruit cake. Not surprisingly, a new book from Chris's fountain pen is eagerly awaited and sought after by both anglers and collectors alike. *The Deepening Pool* (1990), whose central theme concerns fishing for barbel on the Hampshire Avon, has got to be my favourite book of Chris Yates's books. Chris is also a professional photographer and the book is beautifully enhanced by his evocative photographs.

Another modern author, whose books I greatly enjoy, is John Gierach, who hails from across the Pond. He does for American flyfishing what Chris Yates has done for English coarse fishing. He captures the very spirit of flyfishing and distils it in print. Like Yates, Gierach spends much of his time fishing and writing about fishing and even has a penchant for bamboo rods. Unlike Yates, he brews coffee over a camp fire, not tea! I think I now have all of Gierach's books in my collection

(some of them signed) but my favourite is *Trout Bum* (1986), in which he vividly describes the people, the places and the accoutrements that make up his fishing trips.

Although I started out as a coarse angler, nowadays, I mainly fish for trout both in rivers and still-water, with occasional forays after barbel, salmon and pike, and this is reflected in my growing collection of angling books. I also enjoy grayling fishing and I have managed to build up a good selection of grayling classics by Pritt, Walbran, Carter Platts, Roberts (left) and Broughton. Fly dressing is another of my passions and during long winter days I like to dress classic salmon flies and this, too, has led me to branch out into collecting classic salmon fly books. As well as the works of Francis, Kelson and Ephemera, I have eagerly sought out the splendidly produced modern books by Ken Sawada, Paul Schmookler and Ingrid Sils, and Michael D Radencich, which are destined to become the classics of the future. More recently I have built up a collection of books relating to the history of angling and angling art. David Beazley's lavish book, *Images of Angling* (2010), is a must for anyone interested in the visual depiction of angling.

No angling library would be complete without a few editions of Izaak Walton's *Compleat Angler*, first published in 1653 and now running to over five hundred editions. Indeed, apart from the Bible and the works of Shakespeare, it is the most reprinted book in the English language. Dr Rodolphe Coigney, a French resistance hero during the Second World War, amassed one of the best collections of the editions of the *Compleat Angler* before he passed away in 2001. In 1989, he published *Izaak Walton, A New Bibliography 1653-1987*, containing details of more than four hundred and sixty editions. This has become the standard work of reference on Walton and is a collectable volume in its own right. I am pleased to say that I own a copy of the standard edition, which was limited to 540 copies and signed by the author. I would love to own a first edition of the *Compleat Angler* (I do have a facsimile of it) but, lacking the salary

of a premier league football player or merchant banker, this is just a pipe dream. The earliest edition in my library is the first Moses Browne edition of 1750, the first to be published after Walton's death in 1683. I now own about thirty different editions of Walton, but my favourites, without a doubt, are the two Hanborough Parrot Pieces limited editions (right) of 1988 and 1990, abundantly illustrated by the pen and ink line sketches by Wilton

Priestner ARCA. The Penguin edition of 1939, illustrated with wood engravings by the celebrated artist Gertrude Hermes has also much to commend it and is worthy of a place in any collection.

During my years as a book collector I have learnt a few valuable lessons. The first lesson is that he who hesitates is lost. On several occasions when I have dithered over buying a book in a shop or at a book fair, usually through concern over the price, and have gone back later to buy it, invariably it has gone. Secondly, the condition of a book is important. Whenever possible, I try to buy books in the best possible condition, complete with dust wrapper, if the book originally had one. Thirdly, it is important to do research, especially when buying older volumes. By reading book catalogues and searching the internet I get a good idea of how much I can expect to pay for a particular volume and it stops me (most of the time!) from paying over the odds.

It is true that some of the best fishing is done in print and my collection of angling books helps to while away those long winter hours when the weather is too foul to actually go fishing. Collecting angling books has added an extra dimension to angling itself. I have enjoyed the many hours spent rooting around in bookshops or book fairs in search of some elusive tome and I have experienced the thrill of unearthing some hidden gem. During the time I have left to me I hope to continue adding to my collection. However, when most people of my age are thinking of down-sizing their houses, I could do with up-sizing my house to contain my ever expanding angling library!

CHAPTER TWO

Angling Books as History

I own a Kindle and I also collect angling books. A contradiction you might say, but I disagree. I use my Kindle purely for reading fiction; books that I would otherwise dispose of once read. On holiday last summer I was able to download several novels without their weight and bulk filling my suitcase. However, despite the Kindle's obvious attractions there is no substitute for a real book. Books are emblems of a civilised society and are also objects in their own right and, just like pottery, silverware or other objets d'art, they reflect the time when they were produced. In other words, books have history and just as people collect pottery, silverware or even vintage fishing tackle, I collect books, especially angling books and I am fascinated by their history. Even the popular TV programme *Antiques Roadshow* has a book expert to appraise the volumes brought in by the public. At this point in time the book, which for over two thousand years has been the primary source for finding out information, is in a state of flux as this traditional function is increasingly being taken over by electronic means. In this chapter I would like to explore what it is that make books such fascinating artefacts in their own right.

If all that you require from a book is simply the text then its obsolescence seems guaranteed. However, there is far more to a book than simply the text between the covers. Until the mechanisation of the printing process in the nineteenth century all books were unique handcrafted objects. The text was set by hand and the printed sheets

were gathered, folded, sewn and bound. Indeed, no two books from this period are identical. The idea of a uniform binding is a modern one. Early copies of angling classics such as Walton's *Compleat Angler* (1653) or Richard Brookes' *Art of Angling* (1778) display endless variation in their bindings and reflect their owners' tastes and pockets. Many angling bibliophiles like to specialise in collecting the variant bindings of a particular edition. Even today, with the highly mechanised methods of printing, some angling books are printed in two editions, a standard one and a limited edition. The limited edition is often produced on superior paper and with a leather binding, often signed by the author and sometimes with a fly or even a float set into the inside front cover. I have a number of such books in my collection, my favourite being *Flyfishers' Progress*, published by the Flyfishers' Club in 2000 (above), which is beautifully bound in full leather and carries a salmon fly in a sunken mount in the inside front cover. Another book in my collection, *Some of it was Fun* (Medlar Press, 2003), by Hugh Falkus is actually bound in tanned salmon skin. Such books are works of art in their own right and, not surprisingly, command high prices on the antiquarian book market.

'Never judge a book by its cover' may be sound advice but it is not always practised, as publishers well know. Since the middle of the nineteenth century the mass manufacture of books has led to the exploitation of book covers for marketing and representing what lies inside. This started with the use of decorated cloth covers, before the evolution of the dust jacket in the late nineteenth and early twentieth century. The historical importance of the dust jacket has been slow in gaining recognition since many libraries were in the habit of discarding them as trivial things. However, a chronological survey of

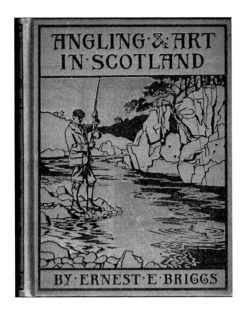

book covers can provide a fascinating insight into changing cultural values and pictorial design. Nowadays, publishers invest heavily in cover design in order to capture the interest of potential buyers and to enforce their brand and identity.

In my collection of angling books, I particularly like the decorative cover of *Angling and Art in Scotland by* Ernest Briggs, published in 1908. The embossed cover, drawn by Briggs himself, portrays an angler playing a salmon on a rocky stretch of river with the sky and water surface picked out in gold. Penguin Books, founded in 1939, was one of the most successful publishers of paperback books in the twentieth century (and is still going strong today). Its success was not just down to cost but also to the smart design of its covers, which were instantly recognisable. The wonderful iconic design of Bernard Venables,' *Mr. Crabtree Goes Fishing*, was no doubt a factor in it selling over two million copies following its publication in 1949.

With regard to dust jackets, very few from before the Second World War have survived the ravages of time but one of the favourites in my collection is the jacket of *Holiday Angling (Mainly for Roach)* by W G Clifford, published in 1925. The design is taken from a painting by Philip Simmond and portrays an angler clad in Tweed jacket and trilby hat sitting by the side of the water contemplating his float. By his side is a wicker creel and a wicker hamper containing his sandwiches and a bottle of beer. It is very much of its time. The 1960s was a fruitful period for angling dust jackets and two of my favourites include Keith Linsell's design for Geoffrey Bucknall's, *Fishing Days* (1966) and Reg Cooke's dramatic illustation of a hooked carp for Richard Walker's, *No Need to Lie* (1964). Both of these books are now highly collectable and copies with original dust jackets, as opposed to facsimiles, can command high prices. Of the more modern books in my collection

I particularly like John Richardson's design for the dust jacket of Simon Smith's, *Running with the Tide*, published by the Medlar Press in 2013. His design features a solitary night-time sea angler bathed in the light of his Tilley lamp overlooking a bay with the lights on the distant shore. It is highly evocative of the book's theme.

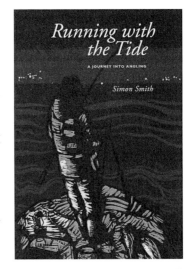

The type and layout of a book is a very important part of book design and nowadays, as I grow older, I automatically tend to reject books printed in a densely packed small typeface. My presbyopic eyes find such books challenging to read! The typeface needs to be of a reasonable size and legible, while the layout must be pleasing to the eye and the finished book needs to be of a size and shape which opens easily and handles comfortably. The books in my collection vary tremendously both in shape and size, ranging from the double elephant folio of Sir William Jardine's, *British Salmonidae* (1979 edition), measuring a whopping 48 x 63 cms to a miniature edition of *Swarbrick's List of Wharfedale Flies*, (2009)

¶ The xxv. chapter shows again another manner of catching many fishes with the angling line.

Item, take a basinful of human blood and half an ounce of saffron and boiled barley flour and unleavened bread, and take also goat's grease that is melted and let it become cold and mix altogether, then take a small piece as big as a nut, and tie it to the line or in a basket as it is most convenient.
¶ The xxvi. chapter shows another manner how many fishes may be caught.
Albertus Magnus writes in his secret book about it thus. Take a few roses and a little mustard and the foot of a weasel, put all that together in a net or in a fish basket and thou shalt

complete with flies inset into the cover. The earliest printed books used gothic-style typefaces, while the letter shapes and type fonts we use today derive ultimately from Roman capitals and the uncial book hands which developed in the post-Roman era.

Of the books in my collection I have several printed in a gothic-style typeface including *Dit Boecxken*, a book on fishing and fowling (left) originally written in Flemish in 1492, but published in a limited edition

24.

THE PIKE.

Scaly, skulking,
lurking, hulking
in your mystic
haunting deep.
Shoulder hunching
muscles bunching,
patient, where the
willows weep.

Eyes a'gleaming,
fins a'streaming,
wary orbs your
vigil keep.
Toothy, grinning,
bent on winning
there, some juicy
meal to reap

English version by the Honey Dun Press in 1978. Alfred Wainwright (1907-1991), the famous Lake District guide writer liked to put his own stamp on his books and they were published entirely as reproductions of his manuscripts. A number of angling writers have followed suit including Donald Downs-Baird (left), Tony Whieldon and Wilton Priestner, all of whom feature in my collection.

Illustrations began to appear in printed books almost as soon as printing began, the earliest example of an illustrated angling book dates from 1496. Some of the earliest illustrations were done on wood blocks, followed by engraved metal plates, either of copper or steel. Colour, if required, was added by hand. During the latter half of the nineteenth century photographs began to appear followed by illustrations printed in colour. Just as book covers and dust jackets provide clues to the dating of books, so too can the illustrations contained within, which reflect changes in artistic fashion. I have a particular interest in illustrated angling books and the subject of fish and fishing lends itself to artistic interpretation. Of the hundreds of illustrated books in my collection I have singled out a few for comment. Joseph Crawhall (1821-1896), a Newcastle ropemaker and keen angler, produced a number of books illustrated with his own distinctive wood-cuts, which were subsequently hand-coloured. Among his works were *The Compleatest*

Angling Booke That Ever Was Writ (1859), *A Collection of Right Merrie Garlands for North Country Anglers* (1864) and my favourite, *Izaak Walton: His Wallet Book* (1885). This latter contains some wonderful hand-coloured wood engravings of anglers in seventeenth century costume, together with numerous vignettes depicting fish, birds, flowers etc (opposite page, below). During the nineteenth

century a number of sumptuously illustrated works on natural history were produced including the Reverend William Houghton's classic, *British Fresh-Water Fishes*, published in 1879. The wonderful colour plates in this book, drawn by the artist A F Lydon, are regarded as the finest pieces of woodblock colour printing of the nineteenth century. Not surprisingly, such is the demand for these plates, that many copies of the book have been broken up and intact copies are now worth hundreds of pounds. P H Emerson was a pioneer of photography and his evocative black and white photographs for the Lea and Dove edition of Izaak Walton's, *Compleat Angler,*

published in 1888, make it one of the most collectable editions of Walton's work. Indeed, the many and various illustrated editions of Walton's classic book are a deserving subject in their own right.

Dumfries and Galloway is one of my favourite parts of Scotland and Ernest Briggs' (1866-1913) delightful watercolours of the area in *Angling and Art in Scotland* (1908) bring back many happy memories of time spent fishing the very waters that Briggs fished during the

later years of the nineteenth century. The interplay of water and light fascinated Briggs and he had a genius for recreating it with a paintbrush. It is a great pity that he died so young. The bibliopolist Ron Coleby was fulsome in his praise of this book, "With clear, well laid-out letterpress and a handsomely decorated cover, this must approach the ideal angling book."

During the period since the Second World War a number of angler-artists have produced beautifully illustrated books including: Bernard Venables, Robin Ade, Robin Armstrong, Chris Turnbull, Maurice Pledger, Paul Cook etc. Their books form an important part of my collection and their style of illustration reflects the period when their books were published.

Once a book rolls off the printing press it takes on its own unique history. Many collectors like to have their books signed by the author and I have many such books in my collection signed by some of the famous anglers of the day. Books are often given as presents and I have a number of presentation copies in my collection including a copy of William Caine's, *An Angler at Large* (1911), which I purchased in Toronto, containing a dedication to Sir Glenholme Falconbridge, Chief Justice of Ontario from 1900-1920, with a long Latin quotation

John A. McKinley

bewailing the passing of youth. There are a number of ways, too, in which people leave traces of their ownership in books, usually by writing their name on the titlepage or by pasting in bookplates. Bookplates vary enormously in their design, often containing family coats of arms or mottoes, and form a fascinating subject in their own right. A number of books in my collection carry bookplates, including ones from bibliophiles John McKinley and the American Jeffrey Norton, whose collection of books on Joseph Crawhall was sold at auction in London in 2002. It is perhaps fitting that the design of his bookplate depicts a trout rising to a fly drawn by Crawhall.

On occasion I have been lucky enough to find books containing letters either to or from the author or containing press cuttings or other items of interest pasted inside. My copy of Robert Sharp's, *Let's Fish the Clyde*, contains a letter to the author written by the Chief Constable of Lanarkshire, while my copy of *Walbran's British Angler* (1889) contains a cutting from the *Yorkshire Evening Post* reporting his drowning at Tanfield on the Ure (right). Some owners like to annotate their

books and one of the previous owners of my copy of C V A Peel's, *Wild Sports in the Outer Hebrides* (1901) clearly disagreed with a great deal the author had written and made some scathing comments in the margins of the text.

Just as there is more to fishing than catching fish, so there is more to a book than the text between its covers although that text can provide us with valuable information or give great pleasure in its reading. Books are physical objects in their own right and, just like other collectibles or *objets d'art*, they have their own history and their design and layout reflect the time when they were produced. Although Kindles and e-books have their place in the greater scheme of things, the world would be a lesser place without the physical book. It is a world I would not wish to live in.

CHAPTER THREE

Antiquarian Angling Books

I am unsure of the exact definition of an antiquarian book, but for the purposes of this chapter, I shall take it to mean a book written before 1900. In my angling library I have a number of such books and, although they were written before 1900, some of the editions in my collection were published much later.

The earliest angling book in the English language is generally considered to be *The Treatyse of Fysshynge wyth an Angle*, published by Wynkyn De Worde at Westminster in 1496. The authorship of this book is attributed to Dame Juliana Berners, who was believed to have been the prioress of Sopwell Nunnery near St Albans in Hertfordshire. This attribution now seems highly unlikely and it is thought that the original manuscript was written in the early years of the fifteenth century. However, the question of authorship does not concern us here. The *Treatyse* is an interesting book in its own right, which gives us a fascinating insight into angling techniques and equipment in use over five hundred years ago. Some of the fishing techniques described seem remarkably modern, such as dead-baiting for pike, a method popularised by Fred J Taylor during the 1960s and 1970s. The list of twelve flies recommended for trout and grayling are not too dissimilar to many of the flies used to catch these fish today, and I have particularly enjoyed dressing a set of these flies from the patterns listed (below). A framed set of them adorns the walls of my study.

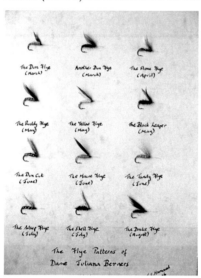

The Dun Flye (March) · Another Dun Flye (March) · The Stone Flye (April) · The Ruddy Flye (May) · The Yellow Flye (May) · The Black Leaper (May) · The Dun Cut (June) · The Mawe Flye (June) · The Tandy Flye (June) · The Waup Flye (July) · The Shell Flye (July) · The Drake Flye (August)

The Flye Patterns of Dame Juliana Berners

A first or second edition of this work (if you could find one) is beyond the reach of most collectors and would likely set you back a six-figure sum, at least. However, a number of editions were produced in the nineteenth century, including a facsimile edition, with an introduction by the Rev M G Watkins, published in 1880 by Elliott Stock. This edition is much more readily available and will not break the bank! Two very important editions of this work have appeared in more recent times and are worthy of a place in the angler's library. The first, containing a modernised version of the text and very useful introduction by angling historian Andrew Herd, was published by the Medlar Press in 1999 and is still in print. In 2001, the Flyfisher's Classic Library published *Dame Juliana: The Angling Treatyse and its Mysteries* with a very useful introduction and notes by Frederick Buller and Hugh Falkus, together with other scholarly contributions. Both of these modern editions are important for the student of angling history.

Without doubt, the rarest English angling book to survive is *The Arte of Angling*, published in 1577. Only one incomplete copy of this work is known to exist and in 1954 it found its way into the possession of a rich American collector who arranged for a facsimile to be published by Princeton University Library (1956 & 1958). In 2000, the

Flyfisher's Classic Library published an edition of this rare work with an introduction by Carl Otto von Kienbusch, the purchaser of the original volume. This book, which is thought to have influenced Izaak Walton, is now believed to have been written by William Samuel, vicar of Godmanchester on the river Great Ouse in Huntingdonshire. The text is in the form of a dialogue between Viator (a traveller) and Piscator (an angler) as is the text of Walton's *Compleat Angler*. The *Arte of Angling* also contains one of the earliest illustrations of a float, made out of quill. This volume is now in the possession of Princeton University Library and is never likely to come up for sale and so the collector will have to make do with a modern facsimile.

Between 1577 and the publication of Walton's *Compleat Angler* in 1653, a number of other books were published, all of which are extremely rare in their original editions. Among the most important of these is Leonard Mascall's, *A Book of Fishing with Hooke and Line*, first published in 1590, which contains much of the same material found in the *Treatyse* apart from a section on fish culture. Mascall, who came from an old Sussex family, was clerk of the kitchen of Matthew Parker, Archbishop of Canterbury. He claimed that a member of his family, 'maister Mascoll of Plumsted in Sussex,' first introduced carp into this country. Four editions of this book were published (1590, 1596, 1600 and 1606) all of which are extremely rare and very expensive. A reprint was published in 1884 by Thomas Satchell and is more accessible to the collector.

In 1613, a long didactic poem on angling known as *The Secrets of Angling* was published in London by Roger Jackson. For a long time the author of this work was unknown but an entry in the Stationers Registers, discovered in 1811, revealed him to be John Dennys of Pucklechurch in Gloucestershire. Seventeenth century editions of this work are extremely rare but a number of editions were brought out in the nineteenth century and in 1970 the Freshet Press of New York brought out a reprint of Thomas Westwood's edition of 1883.

The year 1651 saw the publication of Thomas Barker's *The Art of Angling*. This work is important as it is the first to mention the use of the winch or reel in a reference to trolling for pike. Six years later, an enlarged edition, renamed *Barker's Delight*, describes the use of the reel or winch in angling for salmon. Of Barker himself, we learn from his book that he was born near Shrewsbury, went to London and established himself as a cook. Not surprisingly, given his profession, his book contains a great deal of information on cooking fish as well as catching them. Again, early editions of this work are extremely scarce and correspondingly expensive. However, a number of editions were brought out in the nineteenth century, which are more readily available.

IZAAK WALTON.

No angling library would be complete without at least one or two editions of Izaak Walton's (1593-1683) masterpiece *The Compleat Angler*, first published in 1653. *The Compleat Angler* is the third most widely published book in English literary history following the Bible and the works of Shakespeare. Dr Rudolphe Coigney's *Izaak Walton, A New Bibliography, 1653-1987*, lists over 460 editions. During Walton's own lifetime five editions of the book were published. The most important edition, and the one on which most modern texts are based, was the fifth edition of 1676, entitled *The Universal Angler* which contained, in addition to Walton's text, *Instructions how to angle for a Trout or Grayling in a Clear Stream* by Charles Cotton and *The Experienc'd Angler* by Colonel Robert Venables. Unless you have the salary of a premier league footballer or a merchant banker it is unlikely that you will be able to afford a copy of the first edition of Walton's work. The earliest edition of *The Compleat Angler* in my library is the first Moses Browne edition of 1750 published in London by Henry Kent and illustrated with six copper plate engravings by H Burgh. This edition, the first to be published after Walton's death, came in for a certain amount of criticism for Browne's over-zealous editing of the text. One of the most collectable editions of *The Compleat Angler* is the *Lea and Dove* edition of 1888, edited by R B Marston, which contains photogravures of the rivers Lea and Dove by two pioneering photographers, P H Emerson and George Bankart.

Two other angling books of note were published towards the end of the seventeenth century. The first, *The Angler's Vade Mecum* by James Chetham, was published in 1681 and is particularly useful for its dressings of sixty-four flies. Three editions of this book were published between 1681 and 1700. Chetham (1640-1692) lived at Smedley near Manchester and was a thoroughly practical angler, although his ointments to allure fish to take the bait have raised a few eyebrows since one of his recipes calls for man's fat, cat's fat and finely powdered mummy! The second volume I wish to consider is Robert Nobbes' *The Complete Troller*, published in 1682. This is the first book to be devoted to a single species of fish – the pike, and a single method of fishing for them – trolling. Also included is a brief description of most of the principal rivers of England. My copy of this work is bound together with Thomas Best's *The Art of Angling*, eleventh edition, 1822.

The earliest angling book in my library is a copy of Robert Howlett's *The Angler's Sure Guide,* published in London in 1706. The author was a barrister who claims to have forty years' experience of angling and, although his work is heavily indebted to previous authors, it does contain some original material. He gave considerable thought to the float and its uses and was the first to mention the self-cocking float. His most ingenious idea, however, is for a luminous float made out of a large swan quill containing glow-worms.

The rest of the eighteenth century was not particularly notable for its angling literature although there are two or three authors of interest to the collector. Richard Brookes' *The Art of Angling, Rock and Sea Fishing* proved to be a popular book, which first appeared in 1740 and by 1790 was in its seventh edition and, as a result, is not a difficult book to obtain. Brookes was the first author to mention the use of prawn as a bait for catching salmon and the first to refer to the use of the disgorger. Richard Bowlker's *The Art of Angling, Improved in all its parts, especially Fly-fishing* was first published in 1746 and a second enlarged edition, published in 1774, was largely the work of his son, Charles. The book is especially noteworthy for its section on flyfishing and the natural history of flies and two lists of flies are included. Another very popular angling handbook appeared in 1787 Thomas Best's *A Concise Treatise on the Art of Angling*, which by 1846 had reached its thirteenth edition. In his preface to the

eleventh edition (1822, of which I have a copy) Best claimed that 'since the first publication of this treatise, upwards of twenty-five thousand have been sold.' Many modern angling authors, myself included, would be over the moon if their books sold anywhere near as many as Best's!

The nineteenth century was a period of rapid growth and expansion. The Industrial Revolution was well under way and the landscape of Britain was to change forever. The growth of industry, the spread of urbanisation, and the development of transport systems had a profound effect on people's lives. Angling also underwent rapid change as people sought the solace of rivers, lakes and the newly built canals as a means of escape from their humdrum daily lives. The growing tackle industry and the proliferation of angling books during this period catered for this increased demand.

So many angling books were published during the nineteenth century that it would be impossible to collect them all and the collector needs to decide which areas to concentrate on. In a short chapter such as this it would prove impossible to survey all the angling literature of the nineteenth century and so I shall confine myself to a few general books and books which I find particularly interesting.

At the beginning of the century the Reverend Charles Daniel published his magnum opus, *Rural Sports*, which appeared in 1801-2 (and later editions) and dealt with a variety of field sports, not just angling. It was originally published in three volumes and volume II was devoted to angling. It is sometimes possible to come across these volumes separately and in my library I have a copy of the second volume (in two parts) devoted to angling. It is an extremely comprehensive work on angling and I particularly value my copy for its table of baits and engraved plates of fish.

Another very popular angling handbook of the early nineteenth century was Thomas Salter's *The Angler's Guide*, first published in 1814. By 1841 the book was in its ninth edition. Again, it is worthy of the

PUNT-FISHING.

collector's attention for its fine engravings of fish and fishing scenes, such as 'Punt fishing' illustrated here.

Thomas Hofland (1777-1843) was a noted landscape artist whose *British Angler's Manual* was first published in 1839 and contains 14 steel engravings of paintings by Hofland himself. In my library I have copies of the second (1841) and third edition (1848). The latter edition, published posthumously, contains a memoir of the author by

Edward Jesse together with five additional plates. This book goes to show that sometimes later editions of a particular book are of greater interest. Hofland is perhaps best known today for the artificial fly that bears his name, the 'Hofland's Fancy'.

TWEED FLIES.

During the nineteenth century angling in Scotland was becoming more popular and to cater for that need Thomas Tod Stoddart wrote *The Angler's Companion to the Rivers and Lochs of Scotland*, first published by William Blackwood in 1847. The book, as its name implies, is a very useful guide to fishing in Scotland and contains a beautiful hand coloured pate of Tweed salmon flies. If you fish in Scotland, it is a worthy addition to your library, as are Stoddart's other books.

During the 1780s, Colonel Thomas Thornton, who subsequently became MP for York, undertook a sporting tour through the north of England and Scotland. In 1804, he published an account of this tour entitled *A Sporting Tour through the Northern Parts of England and Great Parts of The Highlands of Scotland*. A revised edition (of which I have a copy), edited by Sir Herbert Maxwell, appeared in 1896. Both editions are now very collectable and give a rare insight into sport in Scotland before it became fashionable in the Victorian era. Of particular interest is Thornton's account of his capture of a 7 lb 3 oz perch in Loch Lomond and his capture of a pike estimated to be around 47-48 lb, from Loch Alvie.

As well as angling in Scotland, I have a particular interest in the fish and fishing of the Lake District and one of the earliest accounts of fishing in this beautiful part of the world is given by Stephen Oliver in his *Scenes and Recollections of Fly-Fishing in Northumberland, Cumberland and Westmorland*, published by Chapman and Hall of London in 1834. The author, whose real name was Andrew Chatto, recommended that in the height of summer, the south-country angler should make an angling tour of the hills of Cumberland and Westmorland and this is precisely what Oliver did and recounts in this slim volume. The book gives a fascinating glimpse into angling in the Lake District before the coming of mass tourism in the

second half of the nineteenth century. Another book of great interest to the Lakeland angler is John Davy's, *The Angler in the Lake District*, published in 1857. Davy was the less well-known, though no less distinguished, brother of Sir Humphry Davy who wrote *Salmonia: or Days of Fly-Fishing* (1828). Both books are worthy of a place in the angler's library.

One of the most important nineteenth century books on fly fishing, *The Practical Angler*, was published in 1857. Its author was a twenty-four year old Scotsman, William Clouston Stewart (1832-1872). As its title implies, Stewart's book was very much focused on the practicalities of flyfishing, as well as fishing the worm and minnow. So highly was it valued by anglers that five editions appeared in Stewart's own lifetime and several reprints have appeared since. Contrary to popular belief, Stewart did not invent upstream wet fly fishing, a number of earlier angling authors, including John Kirkbride of Carlisle in *The Northern Angler* (1837), were urging anglers to 'wade cautiously up the river, and deliver his line well up the stream.' Stewart, however, certainly popularised the upstream cast and favoured short, single-handed rods and the use of sparsely dressed spider patterns. His book still contains a great deal of value to today's angler. Sadly, Stewart died of smallpox at the age of thirty-nine, leaving behind an unfinished manuscript on salmon fishing, which might have proved as popular as his book on trout fishing.

One of the most prolific angling authors of the latter half of the nineteenth century was Harry Cholmondeley-Pennell, who is best known for his *Book of the Pike* (1865) and his two volumes in the Badminton Library, *Fishing: Salmon and Trout* (1885) and *Fishing: Pike and Other Coarse Fish* (1885). All of Pennell's books are worth seeking out.

No angling library would be complete without at least one edition of Francis Francis's *A Book on Angling*, which first appeared in 1867. I own a copy of the fifth edition, published in 1880 and particularly admire the beautiful hand-coloured plates of salmon flies contained within. Francis, like Pennell was a prolific writer and was interested in all aspects of angling and fish culture. Several of his books are in my collection.

I have always had an interest in the relationship between angling and poetry and one of the rarer and more unusual nineteenth century books in my collection is *Shakespeare as an Angler* by the Rev H

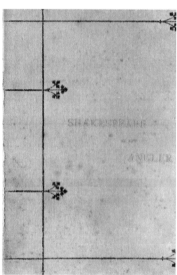

N Ellacombe, published by Elliot Stock in London in 1883. In this slim vellum-bound volume (left), the author examines the references to fish and fishing in Shakespeare's plays and makes out the case that Shakespeare himself must have been an angler.

As a keen grayling angler, there are two nineteenth century books I would not be without, T E Pritt's *The Book of the Grayling*, published in Leeds in 1888 and F M Walbran's *Grayling and How to Catch Them:*

and Recollections of a Sportsman, published in Scarborough in 1895. Pritt was a Lancastrian by birth but spent most of his life in Yorkshire where he fished the rivers of the Dales for trout and grayling. His book contains a wonderful fold-out plate of a grayling painted by the author himself as well as plates illustrating grayling flies and floats. It is a very comprehensive book and is still essential reading for the grayling angler. In addition to his book on grayling, Pritt also wrote an important work on North Country flyfishing, *Yorkshire Trout Flies*, published in 1885. It was republished a year later as *North-Country Flies*. Pritt spent many years researching local fly patterns and his book is an essential reference for the angler who likes to employ North Country soft-hackled trout flies. One of Pritt's friends was Francis Maximilian Walbran, one of the most skilful anglers of the day, who was equally at home on river, sea or loch. His main

passion, however, was for grayling and he made some prodigious catches on the Wharfe and Ure. Sadly, Walbran was drowned while grayling fishing on the Ure at West Tanfield. On 15th February, 1909 he was fishing the rapidly rising river when he encountered difficulties and, despite valiant attempts to rescue him, he was swept away to his death. His book on grayling is a fitting memorial to his memory. After his death, a monument to him was erected in West Tanfield churchyard, paid for by public subscription.

The year 1900 was originally chosen as a fitting date to end this survey of four hundred years of angling literature. It is something of an arbitrary date, however, as a number of authors and their works bridge the nineteenth and twentieth centuries. If you fish the southern chalk streams the works of F M Halford (1844-1914) will be high up on your list of wants. Halford was the doyen of dry fly fishing and his influential book *Floating Flies and How to Dress Them* appeared in 1886, while his *Dry-Fly Fishing in Theory and Practice*, appeared three years later in 1889. His last book *The Dry-Fly Man's Handbook* was published in 1913, just a year before his death.

One of the finest books on flyfishing published during the nineteenth century must surely be Sir Edward Grey's (1862-1933) *Fly-Fishing*, which first appeared in 1899. In the book, the author ranges from his schoolboy days fishing for trout on the Itchen to sea-trout fishing in Shetland and salmon fishing in the north of Scotland. It is beautifully written by the man who was Foreign Secretary at the outbreak of the First World War. Such is the book's appeal that there have been numerous reprints and an enlarged edition by the now Viscount Grey of Fallodon was published in 1930. It is a book that should be on the shelves of every collector of angling books.

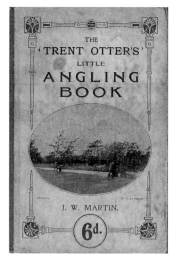

The coarse angler will find much of interest in the works of J W Martin (1852-1915), otherwise known as the 'Trent Otter.' His books, too, bridge the gap between the nineteenth and twentieth centuries. His first book, *Float Fishing and Spinning in the Nottingham Style*, was published in 1882. A stream of books followed, his last being *The Trent Otter's Little Book on Angling*, which appeared in 1910.

Finally, for the angling book collector who is interested in earlier books, published before the twentieth century, the most useful bibliography is Thomas Westwood and Thomas Satchell's *Bibliotheca Piscatoria*, published in 1883. A supplement appeared in 1901 and there have been several modern reprints which combine the two.

CHAPTER FOUR

Collecting Catalogues

During the thirty years or so that I have been collecting angling books I have picked up a number of old tackle catalogues along the way, although they are not the main focus of my collection. Arthur Ransome regarded catalogues as being akin to poetry and "better than books on fishing they transport the reader to the waterside," (*Rod and Line* 1929). He believed they were best read in winter when the weather is not always favourable for fishing. It is also in winter, at the start of the New Year, that traditionally new catalogues began to appear on the shelves of tackle shops, enticing us to part with our hard-earned cash before the new season comes around. The beautifully photographed pictures of fly reels, with the lines lying neatly and evenly on the spools (something that never happens in real life – at least not on my reels!) are extremely tempting. You wonder how you might justify to your wife the purchase of yet another reel when, deep down, you know there is nothing wrong with the old one. A new barbel rod, too, would not go amiss. What leviathans you might catch if you purchased a few of those new spinners and plugs. And so the mind wanders as you flick through page after page of shining new products; it's the child in the sweet shop syndrome! Now, however, the internet has to some extent robbed us of this pleasure and a number of firms no longer produce printed catalogues.

Arthur Ransome's words quoted above were about catalogues of new tackle. Nowadays, there is a growing interest in the collecting

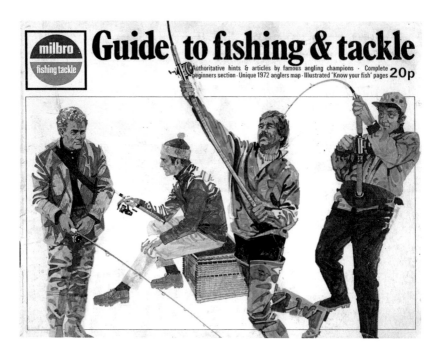

milbro fishing tackle

Guide to fishing & tackle

Authoritative hints & articles by famous angling champions · Complete beginners section · Unique 1972 anglers map · Illustrated 'Know your fish' pages **20p**

of old catalogues and, in some ways, the collection of old fishing-related items is even more compulsive than acquiring new tackle. Nostalgia plays an important part in this. The older I become, the more I look back with fond memories to the days of my childhood when fishing seemed far less complicated than it is now. Equipped with my Milbro solid fibreglass rod, Intrepid reel, a few floats, hooks and weights, I spent many happy hours fishing for perch, roach and the occasional jack pike on my local mill lodge. There was no need of bite alarms, bivvies or bed chairs; fishing was simple. Baits, too, were equally uncomplicated: a few worms dug from the garden, a slice or two of bread or a tin of maggots bought from the local tackle shop. In those days the fishing tackle I bought was all made in the UK not in a Far Eastern sweatshop where the workers are paid a pittance. Old tackle catalogues bring all this old tackle and tackle manufacturers back to life: Allcocks, Milwards, Milbro, Martin James, Albert Smith, Cummins, Percy Wadham to name but a few.

Although you cannot relive the past, I like occasionally to browse through my collection of old catalogues and identify the tackle I wish I had bought back then: a Hardy CC de France fly rod or a Richard Walker Mark IV carp rod, a Match aerial centre-pin or a Jock Scott multiplying reel. My collection of old catalogues proves very useful in identifying and dating the old items of tackle with which I return home after visiting a car boot sale or vintage tackle fair. Catalogues are also a useful tool for researching into the long and fascinating history of our sport.

The fishing tackle industry in this country really began to flourish in the second half of the nineteenth century. Its development was largely fuelled by the growth of the railways, which opened up large areas of hitherto inaccessible countryside to thousands of anglers longing to escape their dreary workaday lives in the industrial towns. During the 1870s and 1880s, as hundreds of angling clubs emerged all over the country, the major tackle manufacturers were not slow to entice these anglers into buying their wares and hence the tackle catalogue was born.

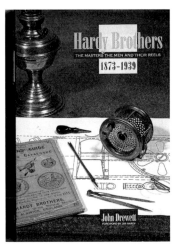

The most numerous catalogues in my collection are *Hardy's Anglers' Guides.* These are also the most valuable and most highly sought after, with early editions now commanding prices of several hundreds of pounds. In 1873, John James Hardy joined his brother William in business at Paikes Street, Alnwick to form Hardy Brothers, which was soon to become the most famous fishing tackle manufacturing business in the world. It appears that the first *Hardy's Anglers' Guide* was produced in 1873 or 1874 and the catalogue of 1883 is described as the eighth edition. In 1889, the firm even produced a catalogue in French, such was the rapid growth of their business. A further French catalogue was published in 1900 for the Paris Exhibition. By their very nature catalogues are ephemeral items

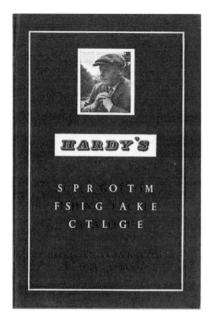

and their survival rate is very low. As a result, catalogues prior to 1900 are extremely rare and correspondingly expensive today. Such is the scarcity of these early editions that John Drewett, author of that magisterial tome *Hardy Brothers, The Masters The Men and Their Reels, 1873-1939* (1998), has published facsimiles of five early catalogues: 1883, 1888, 1894, 1900 and 1905. A complete listing of all known Hardy catalogues is also given in Appendix 4 of Drewett's book. From the 1880s through to 1931 (53rd edition) a full catalogue seems to have been produced most years. In 1932 Hardy introduced a *Super Bottom Fishing Tackle Guide*, which was devoted to coarse fishing tackle. Between 1932 and 1957 eleven editions of this catalogue were produced. A *Big Game Fishing Tackle Guide* was introduced in 1935 and was produced in four editions, ending in 1953, although a *Coarse, Big Game and Sea Fishing Tackle Catalogue* was produced in 1964. During the 1940s no catalogues were produced except for an Export Catalogue in 1948. In 1895 catalogues were sent out by post free to any address on receipt of 3 stamps. Such was the growing popularity of Hardy Brothers and their fishing tackle that, by 1914, twenty-three thousand catalogues were printed and, by the mid-1930s, forty thousand were printed. From 1965 onwards the Hardy catalogues were much reduced in size and are of lesser interest to collectors.

The earliest *Hardy's Anglers' Guide* in my collection is the 1914 edition (right), which ran to over 400 pages and contains an amazing range of tackle from flies to tarpon rods and even boasts a colonial section for ex-pats fishing in India, South Africa, New Zealand or British Columbia. However, my favourite Hardy catalogue has got to be the Coronation Number, pictured opposite, produced to celebrate the coronation of King George VI and Queen Elizabeth in May, 1937. This catalogue has a special cover depicting a portrait of the king and queen. A catalogue with the normal cover was also produced in this year and is much rarer than the Coronation Number.

Reading through a *Hardy's Anglers' Guide* is like reading through a Who's Who of famous anglers, many of whom gave their name to Hardy products. They range from Dr Barton to A H E Wood and from Cholmondeley-Pennell to Richard Walker. Another feature of Hardy catalogues, which I find fascinating, is the number of testimonials from satisfied customers. Arthur Ransome himself commented on this, 'It would seem that no man catches a salmon when fishing for trout without writing to half the tackle-makers bidding them share his joy as the capture was made on this one's gut casts, that one's line, another's minnow tackle and a fourth's dainty rod.' (*Rod and Line,* 1929). A good example is quoted below:

I would like to take this opportunity here of testifying to the quality of your goods, as on my previous trip I landed 49 brown trout on one of your 3X tapered casts without it breaking, also 17 browns on one of your dry flies (Coch-y-bonddu) still undamaged to any extent. S.F.F. (1937 Guide)

Apart from *Hardy's Anglers' Guides,* I have a number of *Allcock's Anglers Guides* in my collection. Like several other tackle manufacturers S. Allcock & Company was located in Redditch and grew out of the needle making industry, which was centred in the town. In 1803, Polycarp Allcock started making fish hooks as a side-line to needle

manufacturing in which he had served his apprenticeship. However, it was Polycarp's son, Samuel, who really developed the fishing tackle side of the business. In

Polycarp Allcock *Samuel Allcock at the age of 30 years*

1851, the company exhibited their wares at the Great Exhibition in London. By 1866, such was the success of Allcock that they moved to the newly built Standard Works in Clive Road, Redditch and by the turn of the century they employed over 400 workers. The company was not destined to survive another century and in 1965 Allcock was taken over by Noris Shakespeare. The following year, two days after Bonfire Night, Standard Works went up in flames and not long afterwards the Allcock name disappeared completely from tackle shops.

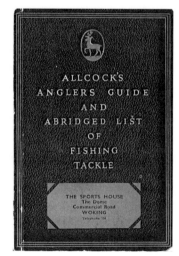

There can be few anglers of my generation who have not owned or still owns some item of Allcock's tackle. Allcock was not quite in the same league as Hardy and their tackle was much more affordable. Perusing their catalogues now takes me back to the

days of my childhood. The first fly rod I ever owned was an Allcock's, made of closely whipped built cane and it was with that rod that I caught my first trout. I also acquired and recently sold a Wallis Wizard bottom rod. This rod was designed by that famous angler of the day, F W K Wallis, who also gave his name to the 'Wallis' cast. Many a tench, crucian carp and roach has fallen to this rod.

The earliest *Allcock's Anglers Guide* in my collection (opposite page, below) dates to 1937-1938, which runs to over two hundred

pages and contains a gorgeous plate of Feathero minnows, one of the most collectable spinning baits today. It also contains one of the most popular of the early threadline reels, the Allcocks Stanley, which is described as ideal for match fishermen 'since it permits them to fish fine and far off.' I once owned a Stanley reel, which I picked up at a local car boot sale. However, like most of the rest of my collection I sold it a few years ago.

Like Hardy, Allcock produced a Coronation Catalogue, but the Allcock one was produced to celebrate the coronation of our present

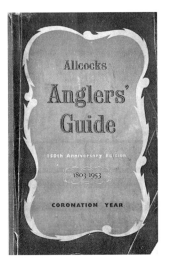

queen in 1953. I came across a copy several years ago at the Redditch Vintage Tackle Fair and it is well worth seeking out since it contains a fascinating history of the company together with a number of photographs portraying members of the Allcock family and the tackle makers at work inside the factory. Like Hardy, Allcock was not slow to include photographs and testimonials from satisfied customers who had caught specimen fish using their equipment.

I have a range of *Allcock's Guides*

dating from 1937 through to their take-over by Noris Shakespeare in the 1960s. One of the earliest *Allcock's Guides* that I have seen dates to 1885 but it appears to have been a catalogue designed for the trade, not the general public. As far as I am aware, the company only started producing catalogues for public distribution during the 1930s.

Some of my favourite catalogues in my collection are the Abu *Tight Lines* catalogues. As a youngster I can well remember looking forward to the arrival of the latest edition in the local tackle shop. *Tight Lines* was always something more than just a catalogue advertising the latest rods, reels and lures. It was a catalogue and magazine combined featuring some of the top names in angling at the time: Dick Walker, Bernard Venables and Billy Lane, to name but a few. To someone whose own angling experiences barely went beyond the canals and mill lodges of Lancashire, *Tight Lines* revealed a whole new world of angling through its reports of the Abu Dream Trips to exotic locations.

In common with several other well-known fishing tackle manufacturers, Abu grew out of another industry, the watch and taximeter industry. AB Urfabriken (Abu) began manufacturing fishing reels at the outbreak of the Second World War in the small factory in the town of Svangsta, on the banks of the famous Morrum River. Such was their success that in 1948 they began publishing an annual catalogue of their wares, *Napp och Nytt*. The first English

version of this catalogue, *Tight Lines*, appeared in 1956 and continued until 2002. By 1966 over a million *Tight Lines* catalogues were being produced every year and were distributed worldwide. The format of the catalogue has changed a little over the years and from 1971 to 1981 the company commissioned well-known Scandinavian artists to design their front covers. Limited edition lithographs of these front covers were offered for sale and are now highly collectable. The 1972 catalogue celebrated the fiftieth anniversary of the founding of AB Urfabriken, by which time the company employed more than 650 people and Abu products were being sold in over 90 countries.

As well as promoting Abu tackle, the *Tight Lines* catalogues included several special features. From 1972-1981, a 'Tide Guide' was printed on the front or back cover, which gave the high tide times for all 365 days of the year at London Bridge. A list of fishing stations around the country was also given, together with the difference in tide times from London Bridge. Equipped with this information, the angler was able to calculate high tide in any area of the country. From the early days of *Tight Lines* through to the 1990s a 'Taking Days Guide' was included, which supposedly gave the angler the best fishing days of each month. Whether it was effective or not, I cannot say, but it certainly made interesting reading. Other useful information included instructions and diagrams of tying knots and advice on filleting and cooking your catch.

During the 1980s Abu, like many other fishing tackle manufacturers, faced increasing competition from cheap Far Eastern imports and was eventually taken over. In 2007, Abu was acquired by the Jarden Corporation of New York. Sadly, the last *Tight Lines* catalogue appeared in 2002, although 2007 witnessed the birth of a new publication, *Tight Lines Journal*, which featured the products of other tackle manufacturers as well as the Abu range. Such was the influence of the *Tight Lines* catalogues that my good friend, David Stanley, and I wrote a book on the history of Abu and its products through its catalogues. *Tight Lines, The Story of Abu*, was published by the Medlar Press in 2007.

Although the main focus of my catalogue collection is on those produced by Abu, Allcock and Hardy, over the years I have acquired a number of catalogues issued by companies that have long since disappeared. These include: Foster Brothers of Ashbourne, Albert Smith of Redditch, Redpath of Kelso to name but a few. Two of my

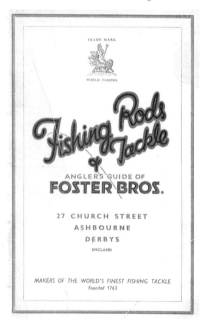

most recent acquisitions include the catalogues of Lee of Pershore and Richard Forshaw of Liverpool. Both of these catalogues date from the 1960s, an important decade in my angling development, and both these catalogues vividly remind me of the fishing tackle I used in my younger days. Indeed, my collection of old tackle catalogues has certainly given me great pleasure and allows me to look back at the changes in fishing tackle during my own angling career and before.

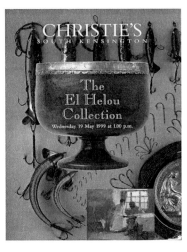

I rarely attend auctions of fishing tackle or books. I do not like the competitive element of these sales and prefer to buy books or tackle from reputable dealers or at angling or book fairs where I can take my time and inspect an item carefully. However, I do have a number of auction catalogues in my collection, mainly of angling books but including one or two of antique tackle. I recently purchased a copy of the Christie's auction catalogue of the El Helou collection, which was auctioned in May,

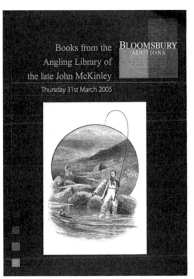

1999. Anissa Helou built up a fine collection of antique fishing tackle and angling art. I did not attend the auction but I purchased the catalogue simply for the beautiful illustrations of the Wyers Freres display cases of tackle that were exhibited in the firm's Paris retail premises. It is a catalogue I like to drool over occasionally!

I also possess a number of catalogues from angling book auctions although I did not attend the sales. These include catalogues of the library of John Simpson (February and June 2005), the library of Jeffrey Norton (December 2001 and May 2002), the Fletcher Robinson collection (February 2004) and the library of the late John McKinley (March 2005). All of these catalogues contain wonderful illustrations of some of the books offered for sale, together with extremely useful bibliographic information and a guide to the value of the books.

Nowadays, I do not actively seek out tackle or angling book catalogues to add to my collection, but, if I come across one at a book or tackle fair, I find it hard to resist and some catalogues can still be picked up relatively cheaply.

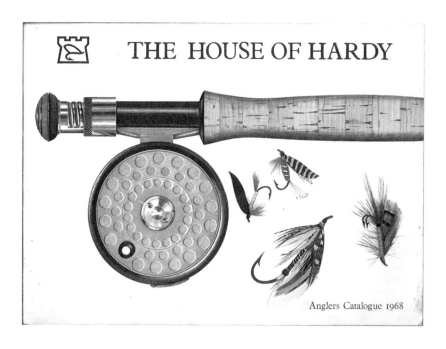

CHAPTER FIVE

Angling Magazines

The trouble with collecting magazines, whether they are angling magazines or other, is that they take up an inordinate amount of space. Unless you have a large house with plenty of storage space or a very understanding wife, you need to be selective in what you collect. I hate to think of the many thousands of pounds I must have spent over the last fifty years or so on buying angling papers and magazines, most of which eventually ended up in the dustbin or, in our more enlightened times, in the recycling bin. This is a great pity since I now realise how important they are in researching the long history of our sport and I wish I had held on to more of them.

At a local car boot sale I recently purchased a large box containing a complete run of *Angling Times* from 1962-1964, formative years in my own angling development. In fact, at that stage in my life, *Angling Times* was delivered weekly to our house and I had probably read and disposed of the same issues that I had just recently bought. As I looked through the fragile yellowing pages I was filled with nostalgia and I enjoyed reading again some of the articles written by once familiar names such as Fred J Taylor, Richard Walker, T K Wilson and Peter Drennan, to name but a few. I was particularly fascinated by the adverts from over fifty years ago and wished I had bought some of the tackle on offer at the time, some of which would now be highly desirable in the collectors' market. Unfortunately, this box of angling papers proved too big to store and so I went through the issues again and cut out the articles and adverts which I thought may be of longer term interest and stored them in a cardboard wallet. The rest of the material went in the recycling bin. I still have a few back copies of *Angling Times* tucked away in my study, including the issue of Wednesday, 25 April, 2001 bearing the headline 'Goodbye Mr Crabtree' and carrying a tribute to Bernard Venables, the co-founder of *Angling Times*, first published on 10 July, 1953.

I still buy *Angling Times* occasionally, as well as *Trout and Salmon*, *Fly Fishing & Fly Tying* and *Improve Your Coarse Fishing* magazines. However, I do not keep hold of them but, if I come across an interesting article or fly pattern I want to keep, I cut it out and file it. This saves a great deal of space! However, I do keep hold of the odd special issue and I have a copy of *Trout and Salmon* from July 2005, the fiftieth anniversary issue.

Some magazines I do keep and, as an all-round angler myself, I particularly like magazines that cater for like-minded anglers. One

of my favourite magazines is *Waterlog* and I have a complete set from the first issue, which appeared in 1996 to the present day. The magazine was founded by Jon Ward-Allen and Chris Yates with the objective of 'providing good quality, albeit eccentric stories in magazine format for anglers who enjoy the process of fishing as much, if not more than the catch.' Originally the magazine was issued bi-monthly but from issue 51 (Spring 2005) it was published quarterly in a different format. I particularly like the magazine for its quality of writing and the range of articles in each issue. Not only does it cater for the game, coarse and sea angler but it also contains articles on the history of angling and environmental issues. It is a genuine all-round angling magazine, which has something for

everyone. I must admit to a certain amount of bias here since I have been a regular contributor to the magazine since 1999. At the end of every year I take my year's copies of *Waterlog* to my local bookbinder and have them bound in a uniform format. They now fill an entire shelf in one of my bookcases.

In 2014, a new magazine designed for the all-round angler

appeared on the block – *Fallon's Angler*. Founded by Garrett Fallon, the magazine is somewhat similar in form and content to *Waterlog* and 'celebrates the telling of the angling story through original, long-form writing with a strong, narrative feel, and avoids the incessant barrage of tackle and tactics.' Many of the contributors to this magazine have also featured in *Waterlog*. As I write this (November 2015), only four issues of the magazine have been published and it is too early to tell of its success or otherwise but it is a magazine I shall collect rather than dispose of once read.

As an angling historian, I was particularly pleased when *Classic Angling* magazine made its first appearance in July 1999. The magazine, edited since the first issue by Keith Elliott, proclaims itself as 'the world's largest full-colour magazine on collecting and using classic tackle, and the history of fishing.' It is a magazine I have subscribed to since the first issue and have found it an invaluable reference work when researching various aspects of angling history or bygone fishing tackle. All my copies are bound by year and sit proudly on my bookshelves alongside my bound copies of *Waterlog*. Unfortunately, over the last couple of years or so I feel the magazine has lost its way a

little and too much of the content is given over to the angling and collecting scene in the USA and abroad, although to be fair, it does have an international readership and perhaps this shift of emphasis reflects its clientele.

Without a doubt the most sumptuous angling magazine ever to appear on the market was the *Art of Angling Journal*, which made its first appearance in the USA in the winter of 2001. The magazine,

published quarterly, was the brainchild of Paul Schmookler and Ingrid Sils, who also acted as editors and were responsible for its art and design. The magazine was printed in Hong Kong and contained stunning colour photography throughout. Indeed, its photographs of trout and salmon flies, both classic and contemporary, have rarely been surpassed. The magazine contained an excellent mixture of articles on fly dressing past and present, contemporary makers of rods and reels, angling artists and reports of worldwide fishing expeditions. Sadly, the magazine only lasted nine issues. I suspect that it was just too expensive to produce. Luckily, I have a complete set. It is a magazine well worth seeking out and back copies do turn up for sale occasionally.

Whilst on the subject of magazines published in the United States, I have been a member of the American Museum of Fly Fishing for a number of years and, as a member, I am entitled to receive copies of its prestigious quarterly journal, *The American Fly Fisher*, which deals with the history of angling both in the United States and elsewhere. Indeed, I have been fortunate enough to have a number of articles published in this journal

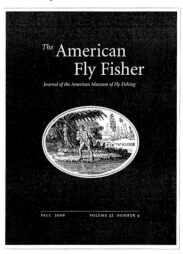

and, as a result, I have a set of bound copies dating back to the winter of 1994. My published articles in this highly respected journal include: Thomas Bewick, the Ramsbottoms pioneers of pisciculture, Sir Herbert Maxwell, Charles Kingsley etc. Like some of the other magazines in my collection, I find myself constantly looking back through issues when carrying out research into aspects of angling history.

At various times during the last forty years I have been a member of a number of specialist angling societies including: the Barbel Society, the Grayling Society, the Pike Anglers' Club, the Fly Dressers' Guild and the Lure Angling Society. All of these societies publish their own journals and over the years I had accumulated a large number of these, some of which had been inserted into binders. They were taking up a great deal of space on my bookshelves and when I retired from full-time employment several years ago I decided to have a clear-out and got rid of the vast majority of them. I now regret selling off my complete run of *Grayling,* the journal of the Grayling Society. However, I did keep

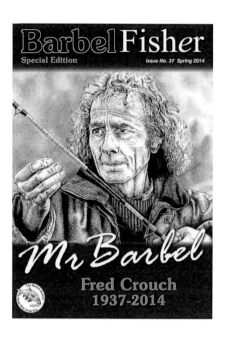

hold of a number of back copies of certain journals including a copy of *Barbel Fisher*, No 37 Spring 2014, which was devoted to the legendary barbel maestro Fred Crouch who had recently passed away.

Although I am not a member of the prestigious Flyfishers' Club of London, which was founded in 1884, I do have copies of the last twenty years' issues of the bi-annual *Flyfishers' Journal*. This journal is highly collectable and contains a variety of articles on the long history

of flyfishing together with accounts of flyfishing the world over. I would certainly not part with these journals and find myself continually looking through their pages when researching articles and books.

The oldest magazine in my collection is a solitary copy of *The Scots Angler* dating from January 1897. As its name implies, the magazine was devoted to angling in Scotland and my copy contains articles on the Murthly Water on the Tay, Loch Shiel and the streams of Perthshire, to name but a few. The adverts, too, are of great interest and the advert for the Clousta Hotel on Shetland is one of the earliest extolling the virtues of trout fishing in those remote islands that I have come across. Sadly, the magazine, which was published bimonthly, only lasted for two years – 1896-1897. Nowadays, copies of this magazine are extremely scarce and rarely come up for sale.

There is one magazine that I wish I had collected when I was younger and that is the *Fishing Gazette*, the longest running specialist angling journal, which was first published in 1877 and closed in 1966. From 1962 to 1966 it was re-named the *Fishing Gazette and Sea Angler*. The magazines contain a wealth of information on all aspects of angling and are an invaluable source of reference for anyone interested in the long history of our sport. The *Fishing Gazette* was published weekly and for a number of years it was possible to buy bound volumes of the magazine issued in twice-yearly parts. These are now highly collectable and command high prices in the second-hand book market. Apart from a few individual issues from various decades I have a bound volume for the months of January to June, 1925. As I glance through its pages it never ceases to amaze me just how geographically diverse some of the articles actually are. My 1925 volume contains articles on fishing from as far afield as the United States and Australia through to Sicily and New Zealand. Some of the earlier years of the magazine dating from the 1890s through to around 1910 can now be found online (www.archive.org) but, unless you have a very large computer screen, they are not particularly easy to read and I much prefer to browse through paper copies. However, in 1997 Swan Hill Press published a compilation of some of the best angling writing from the golden years of the *Fishing Gazette*, 1879-1939. The book entitled *The Bright Stream of Memory* was compiled by Geoffrey Bucknall and is well worth seeking out.

One of the most lavish and iconic angling magazines of the twentieth century must surely be *Creel*, which was launched in July, 1963 and ran until 1967. The magazine, which is now highly collectable, was the brainchild of Bernard Venables. After leaving *Angling Times* following disagreements with Pat Winfrey, its co-founder, Venables wanted a new challenge and that challenge was to create a new angling magazine, not just any magazine, but a magazine produced to the highest standards of the day with colour printing throughout and contributions from some of the best angling writers. The magazine received the financial backing of Wilfred Harvey, Chairman of Purnell, printers and publishers. Venables was the magazine's first editor and, working from his home, he wrote the leader, the diary, his own column, and some of the book and tackle reviews. He acted as sub-editor, was responsible for the page lay-outs and produced a great deal of the artwork. Unfortunately, the magazine was losing money and his publisher began to lose patience with the costs of colour reproduction. Venables produced his last issue as editor in December, 1964. Following his resignation the circulation plummeted and the magazine was eventually taken over by *Angling* magazine but soon afterwards sank into oblivion and the last issue appeared in May 1967. Again, it is a magazine that I wish I had collected more assiduously at the time.

In my collection of angling magazines I have a number of issues of two magazines, both bearing the same title *Angling* but produced by different publishers at different times. The first of these *Angling* magazines was published by Country Life and ran for twenty years from 1936-1956. This booklet-sized magazine was originally published quarterly but, after the Second World War, it was issued bi-monthly. I have a compete volume of issues covering the year from January-December, 1947, together  with a number of individual issues of varying date. One of the longest running features in this magazine was T K Wilson's 'The Story Behind the "Fancy,"' a series of articles devoted to the history of some of the country's best-known fishing flies. The series commenced in July 1944 with the story of that most ubiquitous trout fly the 'Greenwell's Glory' and ended with the sixty-sixth fly in December 1952, the 'Golden Crow,' a less well-known grayling fly devised by Henry Bradshaw of Leeds.

The second magazine bearing the title *Angling* made its first appearance in June 1959 and was published by the Caxton Publishing Company of Welwyn Garden City in Hertfordshire. The magazine, published monthly and edited by Kenneth Mansfield, was aimed at the all-round angler and contained a variety of articles on coarse, game and sea fishing plus reviews of the latest books and tackle. I recently came across a run of issues complete with binder from June 1959-May 1961 in a small bookshop in the Scottish Borders and for which I paid the princely sum of £6. On browsing through its pages I was impressed by the calibre of its contributors whose names read like a Who's Who of the leading anglers of the day: Peter Stone, William B Currie, Bruce McMillen, Eric Horsfall Turner, Tag Barnes, T K Wilson

to name but a few. The magazine ran from 1959-1981 and from 1981-1983 it lived on under a new name *Coarse Fishing Monthly*. Copies of the earlier issues of *Angling* are now very collectable.

The final magazine in my collection, which I would like to consider, is *Fishing*, which was published by EMAP in 1963 and ran until December 1969. The magazine, which was originally published on

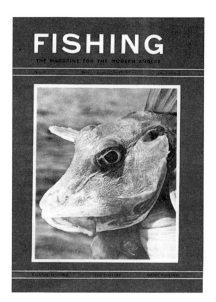

a weekly basis and from 1966 monthly, was a companion to *Angling Times*. The magazine, however, was noted for its in-depth treatment of certain topics and included a long-running series on the design of floats. The magazine, initially edited by Jack Thorndike and in later years by Roy Eaton, attracted some of the leading angling writers of the day. In my angling library I have a set of issues, complete in binders, from January 1963 to December 1969, which I was given by a friend. When I was researching my volume on the history of the float and float fishing, *The Float* (Medlar Press, 2003), I found it an invaluable resource and I still enjoy browsing through its contents today.

Angling magazines are immensely valuable to anyone carrying out research into the long history of our sport. Unfortunately, as we have seen, magazines are ephemeral publications and many have ended up being thrown away or re-cycled. The British Library at its outposts at Collindale in north London and Boston Spa in Yorkshire hold a good collection of angling magazines but by no means a comprehensive collection. Angling historian Kevin Clifford and Angling Heritage in Devon have amassed large collections of angling magazines, which they are willing to make available to serious angling researchers. They also welcome contributions to fill in any gaps in their libraries.

Over the last fifty years or so the number of angling magazines has multiplied, many designed to cater for the new breed of carp and specialist anglers and it would be an impossible task to keep abreast of all of them. The collector, therefore, needs to be selective in choosing which magazines to keep and which to place in the recycling bin. However, before you do dispose of angling magazines think how useful (and possibly valuable) they may be in fifty years' time.

Below is a list of some of the more common angling magazines that have appeared over the last hundred years or so. It is by no means comprehensive.

Title	From	To
The Angler	1948	1956
The Angler's News	1900	1956
Angler's World	1962	1968
Angler's Mail	1964	Present
Angling (Country Life)	1936	1956
Angling (Caxton Publishing)	1959	1981
Angling Telegraph	1963	1976

The American Fly Fisher	1974	Present
The Art of Angling Journal	2001	2005
Big Fish World	1990	1992
Carpworld	1988	Present
Coarse Angler	1977	1992
Coarse Angling Today	2001	Present
Coarse Fisherman	1975	2010
Coarse Fishing Monthly	1981	1983
Classic Angling	1999	Present
Creel	1963	1967
Fallon's Angler	2014	Present
Fishing	1963	1969
Fishing Gazette	1877	1966
Fly Fishing & Fly Tying	1990	Present
Flyfishers' Journal	1911	Present
Improve Your Coarse Fishing	1991	Present
The Midland Angler	1946	1964
Sea Angler	1972	Present
The Scots Angler	1896	1897
Trout and Salmon	1955	Present
Trout Fisherman	1977	Present
Waterlog	1996	Present

CHAPTER SIX

Angling Booklets

Angling booklets are frequently overlooked both by book collectors and booksellers. Like angling magazines and newspapers, they are ephemeral items and I suspect that many of them ended up in the dustbin or recycling bin. As a result, some of them are quite scarce and have become increasingly valuable in the second-hand book market. At book fairs, and even in bookshops, they can often be found apart from the main shelves of books in a wooden or cardboard box. It is well worth rummaging through these boxes as you may stumble upon some unexpected gem which could be worth far more than the asking price. During my time as a collector I have come across quite a number of such treasures and they now form an interesting and valuable part of my collection. Many of these booklets are of a local interest and were published in small numbers. Other booklets were designed to instruct and cover many aspects of angling from fly dressing to spinning for trout or even to choice of float. A number were published by the leading angling newspapers of the day, particularly

Angling Times, and some were given away free as an incentive to buy the newspaper or magazine.

One of the oldest angling booklets in my collection is entitled *The Angler: How, When and Where to Fish*. It was published by Dean & Son of Ludgate Hill in London in, I believe, 1871, and sold for the sum of sixpence. It was one of a series of booklets known as *Dean's Sixpenny Guides*, which covered such diverse topics as rowing and rabbits and their habits. As its title implies, this sixty-two page booklet covers fishing techniques in both river and sea and is beautifully illustrated throughout with black and white woodcuts. Although its front cover is now somewhat faded, it does contain some wonderful adverts for London fishing tackle manufacturers now long since gone including: G Little & Co of Fleet Street and Gowland & Co of Crooked Lane. I cannot remember when and where I bought this but I certainly did not pay very much for it and today, I believe, it is quite scarce and valuable.

During the 1970s, Wolfe Publishing Limited published a series of booklets, which is now highly collectable, entitled the *Catch More* series. The series covered both freshwater and sea fish and each volume concentrated on a particular species written by some of the leading anglers of the day including: Jack Hilton on carp, Barrie Rickards on perch, Fred Wagstaffe on chub and Keith Elliott on bass. The covers of these booklets were beautifully illustrated by Keith Linsell, one of the leading piscatorial artists, and are well worth seeking out for the covers alone.

One of my regular fishing haunts is the river Hodder, which runs through the beautiful Forest of Bowland before entering the Ribble below Great Mitton. One of the largest salmon to come out of its waters during the last one hundred years was a magnificent specimen of 36 ¼ lb, caught by local angler Samuel Walmsley (1876-1971) in October, 1929. In my collection of angling booklets is a short pamphlet containing the reprint of an article from *The Blackburn Times* newspaper of November 23rd, 1929 entitled *Salmon Fishing - A Red Letter Day on the Hodder* in

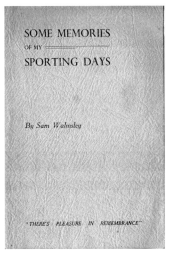

which Walmsley records the capture of his magnificent fish using a 15 ft Hardy cane rod and a *Ballyshannon Parson* fly. In addition, I own a signed copy of another booklet by Samuel Walmsley *Some Memories of my Sporting Days*, privately published by the author in 1949. In it, Walmsley, who was a member of the Whitewell Fishing Association, describes some of his fishing and shooting adventures in the Hodder Valley and beyond. Apart from his salmon fishing prowess, Walmsley was a noted sea-trout angler who has the distinction of having a sea-trout fly named after him, the *Walmsley's Favourite*, a popular choice on the Hodder.

As well as fishing the rivers Hodder and Ribble, I frequently fish a number of Yorkshire rivers, especially the Aire and Wharfe, which are a relatively short drive away. One angler who was very much associated with these Yorkshire waters was the late T K (Tim) Wilson, who passed away suddenly in 1964. As well as being a noted all-round angler, Tim Wilson was also a prolific writer who contributed a great many articles to the leading angling papers and magazines of the day, written in both his own name and under the nom de plume 'Broughton Point.' In 1950, Wilson began writing a series of articles

for the *Yorkshire Evening Post* on angling oddities, amusing tales of fish and fishing illustrated by Richard Taylor, a commercial artist from Skipton. The articles were eventually gathered together and published in booklet format bearing the title *Angler's Scrapbook*. The first booklet was published in 1950 and a second appeared in 1954, both were priced at one shilling. They are now quite difficult to obtain but are well worth seeking out and both contain some fascinating curiosities such as the angling obsessed Coverdale parson who kept a supply of live minnows in the christening font of his church! In addition to the scrapbooks, Wilson also wrote a booklet with the title *The Trout Spinner's Companion*, published in 1952. This booklet, which is not difficult to obtain, deals with the art of spinning for trout with the relatively new fixed spool reel. Although somewhat dated, it contains some interesting information on making celluloid scarabs for fishing the natural minnow and instructions for making quill minnows. Nowadays, I suspect, the booklet is of greater interest to angling historians than practical anglers.

It was Tim Wilson who was responsible for the *Yorkshire Angler's Handbook*, a booklet first published by Dalesman Publishing in 1947, which proved to be a useful guide to fishing localities in Yorkshire.

Two years later, its scope was widened to include waters from Shropshire to the Scottish borders and re-named the *Northern Angler's Handbook*. The booklet was continually updated and ran to at least seventeen editions (1982).

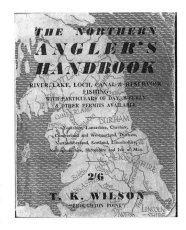

Regional angling guides were, without doubt, the most common angling booklets to be published and in my collection I have numerous guides ranging in geographical scope from Devon and Cornwall to the Orkneys and Shetland. They have proved invaluable when seeking fishing in these areas whilst on holiday. The booklet *Fishing on Mull*, compiled by David Howitt and published by the Staffa Press in 1986, was instrumental in the capture of my first salmon in the river Aros in the summer of 1989 while holidaying on Mull with my family. More recently my wife and I visited Shetland and I managed to glean a great deal of information about the fishing potential of these remote islands from a booklet published in 1967 entitled *Guide to the Shetlands – Game Fishing*.

Although much of the information regarding tackle and contact details is obviously outdated, the lochs themselves have altered very little and I found much of the information regarding them to be still valid.

While carrying out research for my book *Fish and Fishers of the Lake District*, Medlar Press 2014, I came across a great deal of information in guide books to Lakeland angling published during the last fifty years or so. One booklet I found particularly useful was *Reflections Upon Lakeland Angling* (1989) by the late James Holgate, a pike angler of note and former editor of *Pike and Predators* magazine. The Lake District is home to some rare species  of fish, survivors of the last Ice Age, and this booklet contains a mine of information not only on these fish but also on some of the species more commonly targeted by anglers. Sadly, I fear that the era of regional angling booklets is coming to an end. Ownership of waters, contact details and prices for day tickets are constantly changing and, as a result, these angling guides soon become outdated. Nowadays, it is much easier for angling associations and owners of fisheries to place details on the internet and to update them regularly.

Richard (Dick) Walker (1918-1985) was one of the angling greats of the twentieth century who was one of the first to apply scientific thought to angling. He is, perhaps, best remembered for his capture of a 44 lb carp from Redmire in 1952. Through his writing he taught that big fish could be caught by design rather than by accident and changed the face of coarse angling forever. Walker read engineering at Cambridge and, unhappy with the design of many of the fishing rods on the market at the time, he designed and built his own, including the legendary Mark IV carp rod on which he caught his prized fish. Not surprisingly, many anglers wished to build their own rods and to

help them Walker wrote a useful little booklet *Rod Building for Amateurs*, first published in 1952. Unfortunately, I do not own a copy of the much sought after first edition but I do have a copy of the third edition published in 1963, which is still highly collectable.

As well as designing fishing rods and electric bite alarms, Walker also studied the behaviour of fish and in 1959 wrote a very useful booklet, published by *Angling Times*, entitled *How Fish Feed*. The booklet is based on a series of articles Walker wrote for *Angling Times* during the close season of 1958. The articles contained so much original thinking about fish behaviour that it was decided to publish them in book form and it is still a publication that should be read by every thinking angler.

Following Dick Walker's death in 1985, the Carp Society published a tribute in his honour, *Dick Walker: a Memoir* (1988). This booklet, which is now highly sought after, contains several tributes to the great man from his friends and acquaintances including: Chris Yates, Tim Paisley, Colin Willock, Fred Buller, Fred J Taylor and Rod Hutchinson. Also included is Walker's own account of his capture of 'Clarissa,' his 44 lb record carp from Redmire.

Walker was not the only angler to have a booklet published in his honour following his death. In my collection I have a number of such

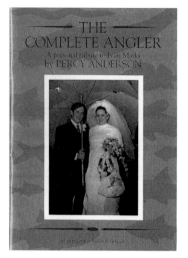

booklets, including tributes to barbel supremo Fred Crouch (1937-2014), all-round angler and author Peter Stone (1927-2000), and (left) match angling legend Ivan Marks (1936-2004). This last booklet is interesting since the sales from its publication were donated to Papworth Hospital in Cambridgeshire where Marks underwent a heart transplant in 1993.

Another category of angling booklet I would like to consider is that of the angling club history. Quite a number of angling clubs and associations have published booklets outlining their histories, mainly for the benefit and interest of past and present members. As a result, most were published in fairly limited numbers and are not often seen for sale. Although I am not a member of the Carlisle Angling Association, I do own a copy of the club's history, written by Edgar Cave and printed during the late 1970s by Thurnams of Carlisle. The Association, founded in 1852, has a long and distinguished history, and controls around seven miles of fishing on the river Eden.

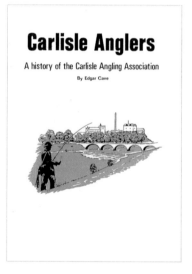

One of my angling acquaintances is a member of the Appletreewick, Barden and Burnsall Angling Club and, over the years, I have had the good fortune to fish as a guest on its hallowed waters on the Wharfe upstream of Bolton Abbey. Founded in 1873, a number of distinguished north-country anglers have been counted among its members including: Francis Max Walbran, Sylvester Lister, Edmunds and Lee of *Brook and River Trouting* (1916)

fame, J H R Bazley and Reg Righyni. I recently managed to purchase copies of the two booklets outlining the club's history – *A Dales Fishing Story*. The first volume, written by John Baker, celebrates the club's centenary and was published in 1973. The second volume by Howard Ratcliffe continues the story from 1973-2013. Both booklets contain a fascinating amount of material relating to north-country angling and are well worth seeking out.

In 2011, the Whitewell Fishing Association celebrated its centenary year and published a booklet, written by Julian Blincoe, celebrating one hundred years of

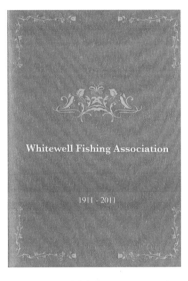

its history. The association controls eight miles of fishing on the beautiful river Hodder, as well as fishing on the river Derwent in Cumbria. I have been fortunate to fish as a guest of one of its members on a number of occasions. The Hodder Valley is an area of outstanding natural beauty and much of the surrounding land is owned by the Duchy of Lancaster. Again, the booklet provides a fascinating glimpse into a little known area of angling history.

The final category of angling booklet I would like to consider is that relating to fishing flies and fly dressing. Jimmy Younger, a professional fly dresser from Torthorwald near Dumfries, started his career with Redpath of Kelso before working for W M Robertson of Glasgow and Sutherland Fly in Helmsdale. His work has featured in many books on fishing and fly dressing and in 1997 he and his wife Gloria published a booklet on fly dressing complete with patterns for over 350 salmon flies. The booklet, entitled *"The Book"* – *Salmon, Trout and Sea-Trout Flies*, contains a wealth of information and advice on tying flies and I find myself turning to it again and again. It is a very useful booklet for the aspiring fly dresser. Another professional fly dresser who wrote a number of booklets on various aspects of

fly dressing was Thomas Clegg. His booklets include: *Tube Flies and How to Make Them* (1962), *The Truth About Fluorescents* (1967) and *Hair and Fur in Fly Dressing*, first published in 1962, with a revised edition coming out in 1969. I own a copy of the latter, complete with a couple of hair wing flies tied by Clegg himself, which were found inside the booklet.

My most recent acquisition is a booklet entitled *Fishing Flies for Upper Teesdale*, compiled and published by Harry Vallack in 2008. Although I do not fish in Upper Teesdale, the booklet is very attractively produced with colour photographs of the flies listed, complete with their dressings. Most of the flies in this booklet would catch fish in any rain-fed river and I suspect this little booklet will become very collectable in the future.

My collection of angling booklets has given me a great deal of pleasure both in their collecting and in the material they contain. It is an area of book collecting where interesting discoveries can still be made and bargains can still be had.

CHAPTER SEVEN

On a Plate

Some book collectors love them, others hate them and prefer their books to be in as pristine a condition as possible. What am I talking about? Bookplates, of course. Personally, I like bookplates and a number of volumes in my library contain them. However, I do not deliberately buy a book simply because it contains an attractive bookplate or the bookplate of some famous previous owner but, if it does, so much the better.

Once a book rolls off the printing press it takes on its own unique history. Many collectors like to have their books signed by the author and I have many such books in my angling library signed by some of the famous anglers of the day including Fred Buller, Hugh Falkus, Fred J Taylor, and Hugh Tempest Sheringham, to name but a few. Indeed, some collectors specialise in signed copies and a copy of a book signed by its author will often add a premium to its second-hand value, especially if the author was a well-known angler. Then there are association copies – these are books signed by someone known to the author, a friend or family member perhaps. Books are often given as presents and I have a number of presentation copies in my collection including a copy of William Caine's *Angler at Large* (1911), which I purchased in Toronto, containing a dedication to Sir Glenholme Falconbridge, Chief Justice of Ontario from 1900-1920, with a long Latin inscription bewailing the passing of youth. There are a number of ways, too, in which people leave traces of their ownership in books,

usually by writing their name on the title page or by pasting in their bookplate.

Bookplates vary hugely in their design, often containing family coats of arms or mottoes and form a fascinating subject in their own right. Many bookplates found in angling books bear illustrations or inscriptions of an angling related nature. The vignettes of Thomas Bewick (1753-1828), the famous Newcastle wood engraver, are often found on bookplates. This is perhaps not surprising since Bewick himself was a keen angler and many of his vignettes, which serve as tail-pieces in his natural history books, are of an angling nature. Not long ago, while visiting the birthplace of Bewick at Cherryburn in Northumberland (now a museum) I purchased a bookplate of John Anderson, originally engraved by Bewick on box-wood. As well as writing his natural history books, Bewick undertook a number of commissions for bookplates, trade cards, tickets and even bar bills. Box-wood is an incredibly hard wood and is ideally suited to the wood engraver's art and illustrations from some of Bewick's original engraved blocks are still being printed today, as the example above shows.

Joseph Crawhall (1821-1896) was another Newcastle angler and wood engraver whose illustrations have sometimes found their way onto bookplates. Although a master rope maker by profession, Crawhall spent much of his leisure time engaged in writing, drawing and wood engraving. He wrote and illustrated a number of idiosyncratic angling books including *The Compleatest Angling Booke That Ever Was Writ* (1859) and *Isaac Walton: His Wallet Booke* (1885), both of which are now highly sought after by angling bibliophiles. Jeffrey Norton, the American bibliophile, who amassed a collection of around four thousand angling books, chose a Crawhall engraving of a trout rising to a fly as his bookplate. The illustration originally appeared in *A Collection of Right Merrie Garlands for North Country Anglers* (1864) edited by Crawhall. It is, perhaps, not surprising that Norton should choose a Crawhall engraving of a trout for his bookplate since he was a great admirer of Crawhall's work and amassed a fine collection of his books, woodblocks and related ephemera, which were auctioned in London in March, 2002. One of the books in my angling library, *Izaak Walton and His Friends* (1904) by Stapleton Martin, comes from the Norton collection and contains his bookplate.

John McKinley, who died in 2002, owned one of the world's finest private libraries of antiquarian angling books, which he amassed over a period of forty years. He was such a dedicated collector that he even took a university course in book binding so that he could restore some of his treasures. My copy of John Davy's *The Angler and his Friend* (1855) carries a McKinley bookplate depicting crossed fly rods together with a creel, fly-book, fly and leaping trout. It is one of the more attractive bookplates in my collection (see page 31).

One of the more unusual bookplates in my angling library is to be found in my copy of Thomas Moule's *Heraldry of Fish* (1842). Rather fittingly, it depicts the heraldic crest of Edward Swinfen Harris, together with a long Latin inscription extolling the virtue of books. From my researches it appears that Swinfen Harris (1841-1924) was a noted architect responsible for the design of the Church of England School (now the Plough Inn) at Stony

Stratford in Buckinghamshire. He appears to have been a native of that town and his memory is preserved in the Swinfen's Court development opposite the school. The Latin quotation beginning *haec studia adulescentiam alunt, senectutem oblectant* ... is taken from Cicero's *Pro Archia* and loosely translates as 'studying in youth sustains delight into old age ...'

Unfortunately, the Swinfen Harris coat of arms does not contain any fish but four creatures that look like wild boar and the faces of several cat-like creatures. I have not yet been able to ascertain whether Swinfen Harris was an angler or simply interested in heraldic design.

It is not just individual collectors who like to stamp their ownership on the books in their collection by inserting bookplates, it used to be common practice for angling clubs and societies to amass small libraries of angling books for use by their members and these invariably contain bookplates. Alas, many of these libraries have since disappeared and been sold off. One of the books in my collection, *Mostly About Trout* (1921) by Sir George Aston, bears the bookplate of the Nottingham Fly Fishers' Club. The bookplate is rather attractive and depicts a river scene with a trout and grayling inset into the design. It appears that the Nottingham Fly Fishers' Club is no longer in existence and its library has been dispersed.

One of the most famous flyfishing clubs still in existence is the prestigious Flyfishers' Club, a gentlemen's club founded in 1884. The club is currently housed in rooms above the Savile Club in London's Brook Street and counts many distinguished fly fishers among its past and present members. The club, too,

THE BOOK-PLATE OF THE FLY-FISHERS' CLUB LIBRARY

is home to a comprehensive library of books on flyfishing, which carry the Club's famous bookplate of a creel replete with books and bearing the Club's motto beneath – *piscator non solum piscatur*, which roughly translates as 'there is more to fishing than catching fish.'

One of the most attractive and ostentatious bookplates in my collection is pasted on the inside front cover of *Fishing Experiences* (1893) by Major F Powell Hopkins. I purchased the book from an antiquarian bookshop in Llandudno a number of years ago but the bookplate is that of Theodore Woodman Gore (1847-1923) who appears to have been a marine adjuster and bibliophile from Boston, Massachusetts. His bookplate, which is reminiscent of  the design of the reverse of an old penny portraying the goddess Britannia complete with shield, depicts a young man bearing a large quill pen in his left hand seated on a pile of books with his right hand resting atop a shield bearing the family motto – *in hoc signo vinces*, which translates as 'under this sign you will prosper.' Unusually for a bookplate it is signed by the artist E H Blashfield (1848-1936). From my researches it appears that Edwin Holland Blashfield was an important American bookplate designer before becoming better known as a painter of marine and figurative subjects. I have not been able to ascertain whether the original owner of the book, Theodore Woodman Gore, was an angler or not. As well as bearing his wonderful bookplate, the book has further interest since it is also associated with his son Samuel (born 1895) and carries his signature and a date of October 31, 1908. Presumably, Mr Gore passed his copy of the book onto his son. How it ended up in a bookshop in Llandudno I do not know!

As well as being attractive to look at and adding interest by way of learning about previous owners, bookplates do have a practical purpose. Just like a library stamp they can serve as a reminder to the borrower that the book is actually the property of someone else. On a number of occasions I have lent a book to a friend and the book has not been returned at all or only after a number of reminders. This brings me on to the final bookplate I would like to consider.

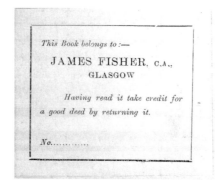

In my copy of *Days and Ways of a Scottish Angler* (1932) by Henry Lamond there is the bookplate of James Fisher C.A., (chartered accountant) of Glasgow. The bookplate is very plain, but typical perhaps of an accountant, contains the following exhortation to the person borrowing it: 'Having read it take credit for a good deed by returning it.' This seems to me a very good idea and a similar plate would not come amiss in my books.

For the collector who would like to have his/her own bookplate there are a number of commercial versions on the market already bearing attractive designs on which the owner simply needs to add his/her name. However, for the serious bibliophile there is nothing like having your own personalised bookplate adorning the inside front cover of your treasured volumes.

Bookplate of Lewis Pendarves Kekewich (1889-1947), a London businessman, in the author's copy of Fishing: Pike and Coarse Fish, *(1896) by H. Cholmondeley-Pennell.*

PART TWO

THE ANGLER'S LIBRARY

MAINLY ABOUT
FISHING

ARTHUR RANSOME

CHAPTER EIGHT

The Angler's Library I

Books on All-round Angling,
on Angling Bibliography & Biography,
on Angling Art & on Collecting Fishing Tackle

Arthur Ransome (1884-1967) is best remembered today for the twelve children's books that he wrote between 1930 and 1947. As a child he spent many happy holidays with his brother and sisters at a farm at the south end of Coniston and it was these holidays which provided him with the inspiration for his most famous book, *Swallows and Amazons* (1930). It was on Coniston that Ransome was first taught to fish by his father, Cyril, a professor of History at Yorkshire College, which later became the University of Leeds. Ransome was also a journalist and between 1913 and 1924 he spent most of his time in Russia, serving as a foreign correspondent for the *Daily News* and from 1919 as the Russian correspondent for the *Manchester Guardian*. In 1924, he returned to Britain and bought a house in the Lake District. He continued to work for the *Guardian* and in the following year introduced a regular fishing column, *Rod and Line*. Fifty of these articles were gathered together and published in a book, *Rod and Line* (1929), which rapidly achieved classic status amongst angling books and ought to be on the bookshelves of every serious angler. In his later years he became interested in salmon flies and their history and even devised the famous *Elver Fly*, which makes use of vulturine guineafowl in its dressing. This interest led to the publication in 1959 of another set of essays, *Mainly About Fishing*, which is a must for anyone interested in the history of the salmon fly. A further collection of Ransome's writing on fishing,

87

Arthur Ransome on Fishing, was published posthumously in 1994, edited by Jeremy Swift.

As well as being a good all-round angler, Ransome developed a keen interest in angling literature and in 1955 he published a little known booklet for the National Book League, entitled *Fishing*. This booklet, under the title of *The Fisherman's Library*, was re-published in 1995 with a preface by Tom Fort by the Flyfisher's Classic Library. Ransome was invited by the National Book League to review the field of angling literature and recommend the books, which he felt should form the nucleus of a fisherman's library. Ransome was very aware of the difficulties of such a task and that any selection was bound to be subjective. However, he persevered with the task since it gave him pleasure to recommend favourite fishing books to his friends.

> *Yet, next to the pleasure of reading a favourite fishing book comes that of persuading a friend to read it too. Many is the book that I have lost by foolishly pressing a friend, whom I wished to convert, to borrow it and to take it away in his pocket.*

I, too, have lost a number of books in similar fashion and, although I am no Arthur Ransome, I thought it might be of interest to update Ransome's list to include books published between 1955 and 2015. In doing this I have followed Ransome's principle of giving a free rein to favouritism. I have followed Ransome in dividing the selected books into categories, although inevitably there is some overlap between them. I have also reorganised and renamed some of his categories, and added new ones on Angling Biographies and Autobiographies, books on Angling Art, and on Collecting Fishing Tackle. Since Ransome published his *Fishing* in 1955 there has been a tremendous growth in the collecting of fishing tackle and a resultant interest in the history of angling and angling personalities. Furthermore, since 1955, new methods of printing have evolved that have led to some beautifully illustrated books by angling artists. Ransome's list was composed entirely of books published in the UK and I, too, have followed that general principle, diverging from it only to bring in a few important fly-tying and historical books.

Finally, I would like to reiterate that any list of angling books is highly subjective and I apologise in advance if I have omitted a reader's favourite books.

ANCIENT & ANTIQUARIAN BOOKS

BARKER, THOMAS
The Art of Angling, 1651.
The second edition (1659) was retitled *Barker's Delight.* There was a reprint in 1887.

BERNERS, DAME JULIANA
The Treatyse of Fysshynge wyth an Angle, Wynkyn De Worde, 1496.
There have been a number of facsimile editions.

BEST, THOMAS
A Concise Treatise on the Art of Angling, 1787.

BOWLKER, RICHARD
The Art of Angling, Improved in all its parts, especially Fly-fishing, 1746.
A second enlarged edition, published in 1774, was largely the work of his son, Charles.

BROOKES, RICHARD
The Art of Angling, Rock and Sea Fishing, Watts, 1740.

CHETHAM, JAMES
The Angler's Vade Mecum, 1681.
Particularly useful for its dressings of sixty-four flies.

CHOLMONDELEY-PENNELL, H
Fishing: Salmon and Trout, The Badminton Library, Longmans, Green & Co., 1885.
The standard work on game fishing in the late 19th century. Contributors include J P Traherne on salmon fishing and H S Hall on chalkstream dry-fly fishing.

DANIEL, REVEREND CHARLES
Rural Sports, 1801-2.
Deals with a variety of field sports - published in three volumes and volume II is devoted to angling.

DAVY, HUMPHRY
Salmonia: or Days of Fly-Fishing, Murray, 1828.

DAVY, JOHN
The Angler in the Lake District,
Longmans, 1857.

DENNYS, JOHN
The Secrets of Angling, Roger
Jackson, 1613.
Freshet Press of New York
published an inexpensive reprint
in 1970.

ELLACOMBE, REV H N
Shakespeare as an Angler, Elliot
Stock, 1883.

FRANCIS, FRANCIS
A Book on Angling, Longmans,
Green & Co., 1867,

HOFLAND, THOMAS
British Angler's Manual, 1839.

HOWLETT, ROBERT
The Angler's Sure Guide, 1706.

KIRKBRIDE, JOHN
The Northern Angler,
Thurnham, 1837.

MASCALL, LEONARD
*A Book of Fishing with Hooke
and Line*, 1590.
Thomas Satchell published a
reprint in 1884.

NOBBES, ROBERT
The Complete Troller, 1682.
This is the first book to be
devoted to a single species of fish
the pike.

OLIVER, STEPHEN
*Scenes and Recollections of Fly-
Fishing in Northumberland,
Cumberland and Westmorland*,
Chapman & Hall, 1834.

OPPIAN
*Oppian, Colluthus,
Tryphiodorus*. With an English
translation by A.W. Mair, Loeb
Classical Library, Heinemann,
1928.
This includes Oppian's
Halieutica, written in the
2nd century AD, the earliest
known fishing book in western
literature.

SALTER, THOMAS
The Angler's Guide, 1814.

SAMUEL, WILLIAM
The Arte of Angling, 1577.
The Flyfisher's Classic Library
published a facsimile in 2000.

STODDART, THOMAS TOD
*The Angler's Companion to the
Rivers and Lochs of Scotland*,
William Blackwood, 1847.
A very useful guide to fishing
in Scotland and contains a
beautiful hand coloured plate of
Tweed salmon flies.

THORNTON, COLONEL
THOMAS
*A Sporting Tour through the
Northern Parts of England and
Great Parts of The Highlands of
Scotland*, 1804.

VENABLES, COLONEL ROBERT
The Experienc'd Angler.
This was appended, together
with Cotton's work on
flyfishing, to the 5th edition of
The Compleat Angler.

WALTON, IZAAK
*The Compleat Angler: or, the
contemplative man's recreation.
Being a discourse of rivers,
fishponds, fish and fishing, not
unworthy the perusal of most
anglers*, Marriot, 1653.
The most famous of angling
books, and despite much
plagiarism (as was the custom
at the time) it is light-hearted,
entertaining and informative
and was hugely successful. The
fifth (1676) and subsequent
editions were expanded to
include a second part, written by
Charles Cotton, on flyfishing;
and a third part, Robert
Venables' *Experienc'd Angler.*
There have been hundreds of
reprints ranging from lavish de
luxe editions to cheap pocket
versions.

APPLIN, ARTHUR
Philandering Angler, Hurst &
Blackett, 1948.

Aston, John
A Dream of Jewelled Fishes,
Aurum, 2007.
The Glorious Uncertainty,
Medlar Press, 2012.
John Aston is an all-round
angler; his books are beautifully
written.

BAILEY, JOHN
*Fishing in the Footsteps of
Mr. Crabtree*. Mr. Crabtree
Publishing, 2012.
A modern day revisiting of
Bernard Venables' classic
Mr. Crabtree Goes Fishing,
beautifully illustrated by Robert
Olssen.

BOOTE, PAUL & WADE,
JEREMY
*Somewhere Down the Crazy
River*, published by the authors
(Sangha Books), 1992.
Angling adventures in India and
Africa in search of mahseer and
goliath tigerfish respectively.

BUCKNALL, GEOFFREY
Fishing Days, Frederick Muller,
1966.
Angling tales from the pen
of this well-known angler
and fly-dresser. This book is
worth buying for the superbly
illustrated dust-jacket by Keith
Linsell.

BULLER, FREDERICK &
FALKUS, HUGH
*Falkus and Buller's Freshwater
Fishing*, Macdonald and Jane's,
1975 and later editions.
Written by two of the greatest
anglers of their generation, this
book gives a comprehensive
coverage of all freshwater
species of fish and includes their
biology, history and angling
methods.

CAINE, WILLIAM
An Angler at Large, Keegan
Paul, 1911.
Fish, Fishing and Fishermen,
Allan, 1927.
Two collections of witty essays
on a variety of fishy subjects,
both game and coarse.

CLARKE, BRIAN
The Stream, Swan Hill, 2000.
Not a fishing book but the story
of a stream and winner of the
BP Natural World Book Prize.
A must for the thoughtful
angler.

FEDDEN, ROMILLY
*Golden Days: from the Fishing
Log of a Painter in Brittany.*
A&C Black, 1919.

FORT, TOM
The Far From Compleat Angler,
Merlin Unwin, 1995.
An amusing collection of
angling stories by the angling
correspondent of the *Financial
Times*.

GAMMON, CLIVE
Hook, Line and Spinner,
Heinemann, 1959.
I Know a Good Place, Swan Hill,
1989.
Castaway, Medlar Press, 2005.
Clive Gammon was a superb
story-teller. In these books
he narrates his experiences in
angling - from his beginnings in
South Wales to his experiences
as an angling journalist
travelling around the world.

GREY, EDWARD
Fly Fishing, Dent, 1899.
Deservedly, one of the most
popular angling books,
beautifully written.

HAIG-BROWN, RODERICK
A River Never Sleeps, Morrow,
1946.
Spanning the author's fishing
life from his childhood on
the English chalkstreams to
the steelhead rivers of British
Columbia. One of the great
classics of angling literature and
a marvellous read.

HARDINGE, OF PENSHURST,
LORD
An Incompleat Angler, Michael
Joseph, 1976.

HARWOOD, J KEITH
*Fish and Fishers of the Lake
District*, Medlar Press, 2014.
Interesting look at the history
of angling in this beautiful part
of the country and some of the
unusual fish inhabiting its waters.

HARWOOD, KEITH
The Angler in Scotland, Medlar
Press, 2015.
A very readable anthology of
fishing stories set in Scotland.

HOPKINS, MAJOR F POWELL
Fishing Experiences of Half a Century: with instructions on the use of the fast reel, Longmans, 1893.

HOPKINS, KENNETH
The Bent Pin, Rigby & Lewis Publishing, 1987.
A beautifully produced anthology of poems about fishing.

HOWITT, DAVID
Fishing on Mull, Staffa Press, 1986.

HUGHES, TED
River, Faber & Faber, 1983.
Not an angling book but a collection of poems celebrating rivers, beautifully illustrated with Peter Keen's atmospheric photographs.

LAMOND, HENRY
Days and Ways of a Scottish Angler, Allan, 1932.

LEES, J A & CLUTTERBUCK, W J
Three in Norway, by Two of Them, Longmans, Green & Co., 1882.
The story of three young Englishmen on a fishing and hunting trip to Jotunheimen in Norway around 1880. One of the funniest and most readable angling/travel books ever

MAUNSELL, G W
The Fisherman's Vade Mecum, Allan, 1933.
"On a fishing expedition this must not be left behind." (Ransome).

MACINTOSH, DONALD
One for the Road, Medlar Press, 2006.
One of the funniest angling books ever written.

RANSOME, ARTHUR
Rod And Line: Essays, together with Aksakov On Fishing, Cape, 1929.
Contains extracts from the works of S.T. Aksakov and Ransome's wonderful angling essays from the Manchester Guardian.

ROBSON, KENNETH (EDITOR)
Flyfishers' Progress: an anthology, The Flyfishers' Club, 2000.

SHERINGHAM, H T
An Angler's Hours, Macmillan,
1905.
An Open Creel, Methuen, 1910.
Two collections of beautifully
written and amusing fishing
essays by an all-round angler.

STREET, DAVID
Fishing in Wild Places, Golden
Grove, 1989.
Delightful tales of fishing
the Celtic fringe, including a
chapter on flyfishing for sea-
trout in Shetland voes.

TRENCH, CHARLES
CHENEVIX
A History of Angling, Hart-
Davis, MacGibbon, 1974.
A very good survey of angling
from prehistoric times to the
present day.

VENABLES, BERNARD
Mr. Crabtree Goes Fishing, Daily
Mirror, 1949.
Bernard Venables' evocative
illustrations and beautifully
written descriptions of the
fishing adventures of Mr.
Crabtree and his young protégé,
Peter, inspired a generation of
anglers. A surprising omission
from Ransome's original list.

VOSS BARK, CONRAD
The Encyclopaedia of Fly Fishing,
Batsford, 1986.
A great reference work on all
aspects of flyfishing.

WALKER, RICHARD
Dick Walker: A Memoir, the
Carp Society, 1988.
A tribute to Walker, published
after his death by the Carp
Society, with contributions by
many well-known anglers.

WATKINS-PITCHFORD, DENYS
The Fisherman's Bedside Book,
compiled by "BB," Eyre &
Spottiswoode, 1945.
"A most pleasing anthology
by authors old and new,
particularly of the captures of
big fish." (Hampton).

WIGGIN, MAURICE (EDITOR)
The Angler's Bedside Book,
Batsford, 1965.
Compiled by Maurice Wiggin,
this is a terrific collection of
original writing from all of
the great writers of the 1960s.
Bernard Venables, Dick Walker,
Fred J Taylor, Oliver Kite, C V
Hancock, Jack Hargreaves and
Frank Sawyer are among the
twenty-six contributors. Hugh

Falkus's short story, *The Sea Trout*, made its first appearance here.

WILSON, T K
Yorkshire Angler's Handbook, Dalesman, 1947 & many subsequent editions.

WILSON, T K
Angler's Scrapbook: a series of sketches dealing with angling curiosities, the Yorkshire Evening Post, 1950.
Angler's Scrapbook: second series, the Yorkshire Evening Post, 1954.

ANGLING BIBLIOGRAPHY

BULLER, FREDERICK & FALKUS, HUGH
Dame Juliana: The Angling Treatyse and its Mysteries, Flyfisher's Classic Library, 2001.

CALLAHAN, KEN & MORGAN, PAUL
Hampton's Angling Bibliography: Fishing Books 1881-1949, The Three Beards' Press, 2008.
J F Hampton's 1947 bibliography, updated and expanded by two well-known bibliophiles and booksellers.

COIGNEY, RODOLPHE L
Izaak Walton, A New Bibliography 1653-1987, Cummins, 1989.

COLEBY, R J W
Regional Angling Literature, published by the author, 1979. A useful checklist of the angling literature of Northern England, Scotland, Wales and Ireland.

HAMPTON, J F
Modern Angling Bibliography: Books published on angling, fisheries and fish culture from 1881 to 1945, Herbert Jenkins, 1947.

GINGRICH, ARNOLD
The Fishing in Print: a guided tour through five centuries of angling literature, Winchester, 1974.

HILLS, J W
A History of Fly Fishing for Trout, Allan, 1921.
A good guide to the early angling literature of Britain and of France, with a useful bibliography of English and French angling books.

MORGAN, PAUL
British Angling Books 1870-1970: a Bibliography, Coch-y-Bonddu Books, 2017.
Not yet published, but my publisher never misses an opportunity to advertise! With around 4000 entries to date, it will be the largest and most comprehensive angling bibliography ever, and should prove invaluable for the collector.

RANSOME, ARTHUR
Fishing: National Book League Reader's Guides, Cambridge, 1955.
Republished by the Flyfisher's Classic Library as *The Fisherman's Library* in 1995

ROBB, JAMES
Notable Angling Literature, Herbert Jenkins, 1947.

THACHER, CHARLES
Angling Books: A Guide for Collectors, Meadow Run Press, 2007.
This really useful guide lists over 15,000 angling books that have been offered for sale at auction and by booksellers between 1999 and 2006, together with prices.

TURRELL, W J
Ancient Angling Authors, Gurney & Jackson, 1910.

WESTWOOD, THOMAS & SATCHELL, THOMAS
Bibliotheca Piscatoria, Satchell, 1883.
Together with the supplement, published in 1901, this is the most useful reference to early angling books, giving brief details of almost every angling book published up until the turn of the twentieth century.

ANGLING BIOGRAPHY AND AUTOBIOGRAPHY

FALKUS, HUGH
The Stolen Years, Museum Press, 1965.
Some of it was Fun, Medlar Press, 2003.
The first tells the story of the author's boyhood years and wartime experiences, continued in the second.

GODDARD, JOHN
The Passionate Angler, Medlar Press, 2008.
The very readable autobiography of a far-travelled angler.

GREENHALGH, MALCOLM
Casting a Line, Medlar Press, 2014.
Malcolm Greenhalgh is a natural raconteur and his autobiography is extremely entertaining.

HAYTER, TONY
F M Halford and the Dry-Fly Revolution, Hale, 2002.
G E M Skues: The Man of the Nymph, Hale, 2013.
Thorough and very readable biographies of two great figures in the history of flyfishing.

HERD, ANDREW
Angling Giants: Anglers Who Made History, Medlar Press, 2010.
Short biographies of many of the great names in angling history. A valuable reference.

KNOWLES, CHRISTOPHER
Orange Otter, Medlar Press, 2006.
An interesting biography of the Rev. Edward Powell, outstanding angler and fly-dresser.

NEWTON, CHRIS
Hugh Falkus: A Life on the Edge, Medlar Press, 2007.
One of the best biographies I have ever read and destined to become a classic of its genre.

OGLESBY, ARTHUR
Reeling In, Crowood, 1988.
The autobiography of one of the greatest salmon anglers of his generation.

QUINN, TOM
BB Remembered, Swan Hill, 2006.
A fascinating insight into the life of Denys Watkins-Pitchford, one of angling's best-loved writers.

RICKARDS, BARRIE
Richard Walker: Biography of an Angling Legend, Medlar Press, 2007.
As the title suggests, Rickards concentrates on Walker's angling achievements. Other aspects of his life remain to be documented.

RITZ, CHARLES
A Fly Fisher's Life, Reinhardt, 1959.
Much of the book is on technique, especially Ritz's famous "High speed - high line" method of casting. His reminiscences of fishing, especially in Europe, make wonderful reading.

VENABLES, BERNARD
A Stream of Life, Medlar Press, 2002.
The autobiography of Bernard Venables, written in the author's rather quirky prose.

WADDINGTON, RICHARD
Richard Waddington, 1910-1999, Autobiography, published by Janet Waddington, 2004.
An interesting and well-illustrated account of the life and times of one of the twentieth century's most successful salmon anglers.

WILLIAMS, TOM
A River for All Seasons, Cassell, 1980.
A delightful collection of stories from a Hampshire Avon river-keeper.

ADE, ROBIN
Fisher in the Hills: A Season in Galloway, Deutsch, 1985.
A season's trout fishing in Galloway, beautifully recorded by artist, Robin Ade.

ARMSTRONG, ROBIN
The Painted Stream: a River Warden's Life, Dent, 1985.
Split-Cane and Sable, Dent, 1988.
Beautifully illustrated books by Robin Armstrong, artist, tackle-collector and former river warden.

BAILEY, JOHN & DETERDING, SHIRLEY
Rivers of Joy, Creel Publishing, 1992.
A celebration of rivers through the paintings of Shirley Deterding and text of John Bailey.

BEAZLEY, DAVID
Images of Angling, Creel Press, 2010.
A handsome and scholarly book covering three centuries of angling prints.

BRIGGS, ERNEST E
Angling and Art in Scotland, some fishing experiences related and illustrated, Longmans, Green & Co., 1908.
Combining two of my major interests, angling and art, Briggs' reminiscences are illustrated with his excellent colour paintings and black & white vignettes.

CRAWHALL, JOSEPH
The Compleatest Angling Booke That Ever Was Writ, published by the author, (1859)
A Collection of Right Merrie Garlands for North Country Anglers, Rutland, 1864.
Izaak Walton: His Wallet Book, Sampson Low, 1885.
Illustrated with beautiful and distinctive woodcuts, some hand-coloured.

DOWNES, STEPHEN & KNOWELDEN, MARTIN
The New Compleat Angler, Orbis, 1983.
This book, highly regarded by Dick Walker, is worth buying for the beautiful illustrations by artist Martin Knowelden.

GREENBURY, JUDITH
Spey Portrait, Sansom & Co.,
1997.
This is a personal memoir of
fishing and painting on the Spey
between 1974 and 1989.

HOUGHTON, REV. WILLIAM
British Fresh-Water Fishes,
MacKenzie, 1879.
Written and painted for
anglers, in two volumes, folio
in size, with 41 wonderful
chromolithographs (colour-
printed engraved plates) by A F
Lydon, this is the cornerstone of
any collection of angling art.

JARDINE, SIR WILLIAM
British Salmonidae, Lizars,
1841.
With twelve wonderful hand-
coloured folio plates, this is
worth a fortune! Even the 1979
reprint is scarce and expensive.

MCPHAIL, RODGER
Fishing Season, Swan Hill, 1990.
A fishing season as seen through
the eyes of one of the country's
leading wildlife artists.
His earlier *Open Season*, Airlife,
1986 is also a worthy addition
to the angler's library.

MEERS, TONY
The Angling Artists, Harper,
2013.
Concentrates on modern
anglers, mostly coarse
fishermen, who are also artists.
The contributors talk about
their fishing experiences as well
as their art.

MILLER, DAVID
Beneath the Surface, Langford
Press, 2007.
A stunning book depicting life
beneath the surface by a very
talented fish painter.

PERKINS, BENJAMIN
At the Water's Edge, Viking,
1989.
From the Tweed to the Test
the author fishes and paints
throughout Britain.

PLEDGER, MAURICE
*While my Float's Still Cocked:
the ramblings of an artist-angler,*
Coch-y-Bonddu Books, 2011.
Water Colours, Coch-y-Bonddu
Books, 2013.

QUINN, TOM
Angling in Art, Sportsman's Press, 1991.
This book charts the history of angling in art from prehistoric times to the present day. An essential reference work.

SEE-PAYNTON, COLIN
Air and Water, Medlar Press, 2006.
A celebration of fish and birds as seen through the eyes of wood-engraver Colin See-Paynton with suitably chosen text selected by Keith Harwood. A beautiful book.

SPARROW, W SHAW
Angling in British Art through Five Centuries, Lane, 1923.
A massive, lavish and very useful book.

VENABLES, BERNARD
Bernard Venables: The Illustrated Memoirs of a Fisherman, Merlin Unwin, 1993.
Bernard Venables looks back at his life in angling, illustrated with his own paintings.

WALKER, RICHARD
No Need to Lie, Angling Times, 1964.
Great fishing writing raised to a new level by the beautiful and evocative paintings of Reg Cooke.

FISHING TACKLE COLLECTING

CALABI, SILVIO
The Collector's Guide to Antique Fishing Tackle, Wellfleet Press, 1989.
Dealing mainly with American tackle but worth buying for the beautiful illustrations.

DELLA MURA, JEFF
Hooked on Floats 1860 1960, published by the author (Timbo Books), 2012.
Definitely a book for the float enthusiast with stunning pictures of floats.

DOWDEN, NIGEL
Old Fishing Tackle, Shire
Publications, 1995.
A good and reasonably priced
introduction to old fishing
tackle.

DREWETT, JOHN
*Hardy Brothers: The Masters
The Men and Their Reels, 1873-
1939*, published by the author
(J&J Publishing), 1998.
A stunning and comprehensive
book on Hardy reels.

HARDY, JAMES LEIGHTON
*The House the Hardy Brothers
Built*, Flyfisher's Classic Library,
1998.
A history of the famous tackle
firm written by a member of the
Hardy family.

HARWOOD, J KEITH
The Float, Medlar Press, 2003.
*The Hardy Book of the Salmon
Fly*, Medlar Press, 2006.

HARWOOD, J KEITH AND
STANLEY, DAVID
Tight Lines: the Story of Abu,
Medlar Press, 2007.
An attractively produced book
on the history of Abu.

HARWOOD, J KEITH, HERD,
ANDREW & STANLEY, DAVID
*Gear and Gadgets: An Irresistible
Collection of Hardy Fishing
Tackle*, Medlar Press, 2012.
Dealing with some of the
angling accessories offered for
sale by Hardy Brothers.

HERD, ANDREW
*The History of Fly Fishing:
Volume I The History, Volume II
Trout Fly Patterns,
Volume III Salmon Fly Patterns,*
Medlar Press, 2011, 2012 & 2013.
Hardy Anglers' Bible, Medlar
Press, 2015.
A glimpse into Hardy catalogues
from the firm's inception to 1914.

HURUM, HANS JORGEN
*A History of the Fish Hook and
the story of Mustad, the hook
maker*, A&C Black, 1977.
A fascinating insight into
that most essential item of the
angler's equipment.

KEWLEY, CHARLES &
FARRAR, HOWARD
Fishing Tackle for Collectors,
Sotheby's, 1987.
A lovely book on fishing tackle
collecting and a collector's item
in its own right.

MAXTONE GRAHAM, JAMIE
The Best of Hardy Anglers' Guides,
Macdonald Publishers, 1982.
To Catch a Fisherman,
published by the author, 1984.
A collection of fishing tackle
patents from 1857-1950. A book
for the serious collector.
*Fishing Tackle of Yesterday: A
Collector's Guide,* published by
the author, 1989.

MILLER, JESS
*Antique Fishing Tackle: Hardy
Reels: The Dunkeld Collection,*
published by the author, 1987.
*The Dunkeld Collection, Hardy
Reels,* published by the author,
2004.
A very large format paperback
catalogue containing excellent
photographs of Hardy reels. The
2nd edition, in a rather smaller
format, contains a useful section
on Hardy lures.

NADELL, MICHAEL
*Poles Apart: A History of the
London Roach Pole,*
Coch-y-Bonddu Books, 2013.
A fascinating and beautifully
produced book on the London
roach pole.

SANDFORD, CHRIS
The Best of British Baits,
published by the author, 1997.
A beautiful book with stunning
photographs of artificial lures
from 1849-1930.

SKUPIEN, DANIEL
Vintage Fishing Reels of Sweden,
Schiffer, 2002.
Contains lots of coloured
photographs of Swedish reels.

STANLEY, DAVID
The Hardy Book of the Reel,
Medlar Press, 2010.
A very useful and handy guide
to identifying Hardy reels. A
must for the collector.

STEPHENSON, JOHN
Understanding Threadlines,
published by the author, 1992.
Rosewood to Revolution,
published by the author, 1993.
Two excellent guides for
reel collectors: the first on
threadline (or fixed-spool) reels,
and the second on wooden reels.

TURNER, GRAHAM
*Fishing Tackle: The Ultimate
Collector's Guide,* MPress, 2009.
The standard reference work on
collecting antique fishing tackle.

WALLER, PHIL
Fishing Reels: Collecting for All,
Volumes I and II, published by
the author, 1993 & 2002.
Two very useful guides to
identifying reels.

CHAPTER NINE

The Angler's Library II

Game Fishing and Fly Tying Books

TROUT FISHING

ASTON, SIR GEORGE
Mostly About Trout. Allen &
Unwin, 1921.

BAKER, JOHN
*A Dales Fishing Story: the
Appletreewick, Barden &
Burnsall Angling Club from
1873 to 1973*, published by the
club, 1973.
A second volume was edited by
Howard Ratcliffe in 2013.

BEER, JON
Gone Fishing, Aurum Press, 2001
The Trout and I, Aurum Press,
2003.
A collection of stories in pursuit
of wild trout from the columnist
of *The Daily Telegraph*.

CATLOW, LAWRENCE
Once a Flyfisher, Merlin Unwin
Books, 2001.
The author is a former Classics
master at Sedbergh School,
and this is his diary recording
his trout fishing on northern
rivers. All of Catlow's books are
worthy of a place on the shelves
of the angler.

CLARKE, BRIAN
The Pursuit of Stillwater Trout,
A&C Black, 1975.
This book marked the transition
of stillwater trout fishing in
Britain from traditional loch-
style to modern imitative
methods. A milestone in
angling literature.

FOGG, ROGER
The Art of the Wet Fly, A&C
Black, 1979.
Wet-Fly Tying and Fishing,
Crowood, 2009.

GREENE, H PLUNKET
Where the Bright Waters Meet,
Allan, 1924.
"…an outstanding angling
autobiography, which is quite
rightly regarded as a classic of
the chalk-streams." (Howard
Marshall in his introduction to
the 1969 edition).

GREENHALGH, MALCOLM
Trout Fishing In Rivers,
Witherby, 1987.
One of the best introductions to
river flyfishing, especially if you
fish northern rivers.

GREER, RON
Ferox Trout and Arctic Charr,
Swan Hill, 1995.
Ron Greer is a biologist and a
founding member of Ferox 85, a
group of anglers specialising in
capturing large wild trout from
lochs and lakes.

HAYES, PETER
*Fly Fishing Outside the Box:
Emerging Heresies*, Coch-y-
Bonddu Books, 2013.
Hayes challenges many of the
long-held flyfishing assumptions
and advances our understanding
of how trout feed and how that
relates to the design of flies.

HEADLEY, STAN
The Loch Fisher's Bible, Hale,
2005.
This is a must for anyone fishing
the Scottish lochs.

HILLS, J W
A Summer on the Test, Allan,
1930.
"…conveys the very essence
of chalk-stream fishing."
(Ransome).

IVENS T C
Still Water Fly Fishing,
Verschoyle, 1952.

JARDINE, CHARLES
*The Sotheby's Guide to Fly-
Fishing for Trout*, Dorling
Kindersley, 1991.
A beautifully illustrated and
well-explained introduction to
all aspects of trout fishing.

KINGSMILL MOORE, T C
A Man May Fish, Herbert
Jenkins, 1960.
One of the classic books about
trout and sea-trout fishing in
Ireland.

KITE, OLIVER
Nymph Fishing in Practice,
Herbert Jenkins, 1963.
A Fisherman's Diary, Deutsch,
1969.

NELSON, WILLIAM
*Fishing in Eden: A record of fifty
years with rod and line in the
valleys of the Eden and Eamont;
to which are added some
practical notes on flies and tackle.*
Witherby, 1922.

PATTERSON, NEIL
Chalkstream Chronicle, Merlin
Unwin Books, 1995.
Flyfisher's Chronicle, Constable,
2015.
A thoughtful fly-tyer and angler
tells of his life on an English
chalkstream, and of his angling
travels around the world,
especially in South America.

RANGELEY-WILSON, CHARLES
*Chalkstream: In Praise of the
Ultimate River*, Medlar Press
Press, 2005.
A delightful anthology
celebrating the glory of the
chalkstreams.

RATCLIFFE, HOWARD
*A Dales Fishing Story: the
Appletreewick, Barden &
Burnsall Angling Club from
1973 to 2013*, published by the
club, 2013.
Continues the history published
by John Baker in 1973.

SAWYER, FRANK
Keeper of the Stream, A & C
Black, 1952.
Nymphs and the Trout, Stanley
Paul, 1958.
Frank Sawyer, who died in
1980, spent most of his life as a
river keeper on the River Avon,
where he was instrumental in
developing the modern method
of nymph fishing.

Skues, G E M
Minor Tactics of the Chalk Stream, Black, 1910.
The Way of a Trout with a Fly, Black, 1921.
Side-lines, Side-lights and Reflections, Seeley Service, 1932.
Nymph Fishing For Chalk Stream Trout, Black, 1939.
Silk, Fur And Feather. The trout-fly dresser's year, By "V.C." The Fishing Gazette, 1950
Itchen Memories, Herbert Jenkins, 1951.
Skues's first book "put an end to the dry-fly purist and brought the angling world back to sanity." (Robb).

Smith, Roger S D
Flyfishing the Welsh Borderlands: a review of flyfishing and flies for wild trout and grayling in the rivers, brooks and streams of the region, Coch-y-Bonddu Books, 2011.

Stewart, W C
The Practical Angler: or the art of trout fishing, more particularly applied to clear water, A&C Black, 1857.

Taverner, Eric
Trout Fishing from all Angles, Seeley Service, 1929.
An encyclopaedic volume in the Lonsdale Library series.

Tod, E M
Wet Fly Fishing Treated Methodically, Sampson Low & Co., 1903
A useful treatise on the use of the traditional wet-fly on the streams and rivers of Scotland and the Borders.

Wilson, Dermot
Fishing the Dry Fly, A&C Black, 1970.
One of the best introductions to dry-fly fishing.

Wilson, T K
The Trout Spinner's Companion, Skipton Printers, 1952.
Trout By All Means, Angling Times, 1966.

BROUGHTON, RONALD
Grayling: The Fourth Game Fish, Crowood, 1989.
The Complete Book of the Grayling, Hale, 2000.
The latter book is a completely revised and expanded edition of the former. Both books provide a very comprehensive coverage of the grayling and grayling fishing.

CARTER PLATTS, W
Grayling Fishing, Black, 1939.

KRIVANEC, KAREL
Czech Nymph and Other Related Fly Fishing Methods, published by the author, 2007.
Since its first appearance in this country in the 1990 World Fly Fishing Championships, Czech nymphing has proved a deadly technique for grayling.

MORGAN, PAUL
The Lady of the Stream, Medlar Press, 2003.
A very good anthology of grayling literature by one of the country's leading angling booksellers.

PRITT, T E
The Book of the Grayling, Goodall & Suddick, 1888.

RIGHYNI, R V
GRAYLING, MACDONALD, 1968.
Reg Righyni was one of the founding fathers of the Grayling Society; his book was very influential in popularising grayling fishing.

ROBERTS, JOHN
The Grayling Angler, Witherby, 1982.
Fly Fishing for Grayling, Excellent Press, 1999.

ROLT, H A
Grayling Fishing in South Country Streams, Sampson Low & Co., 1905.

WALBRAN, F M
Grayling and How to Catch Them, "The Angler," 1895.

BRIDGETT, R C
Sea-Trout Fishing, Herbert
Jenkins, 1929.

BLUETT, JEFFERY
*Sea Trout and Occasional
Salmon*, Cassell, 1948.
The first book to discuss in
detail the modern method of
flyfishing for sea-trout at night.

CHRYSTAL, R A
Angling Theories and Methods,
Herbert Jenkins, 1927.
*Angling at Lochboisdale, South
Uist. Notes on an angling journal
1882-1937*, Witherby, 1939.

CLAPHAM, RICHARD
*Fishing for Sea Trout in Tidal
Water*, Oliver & Boyd, 1950.
"...deals principally with fishing on
the tidal waters of the Lancashire
Leven, a stream which runs from
Lake Windermere to the sea." (*The
Scottish Angler,* 1951).

FALKUS, HUGH
*Sea Trout Fishing: A Guide to
Success*, Witherby, 1962.
A revised and expanded version
was published in 1975. The
classic work on sea-trout fishing.

FALKUS, HUGH
The Sea Trout, Witherby, 1987.
A delightful story of the
author's encounter with a large
sea-trout. First published in
Maurice Wiggin's *Angler's
Bedside Book*, 1965, it was
re-issued as a limited edition
in 1987 to commemorate the
author's 70th year and the 25th
anniversary of the publication of
Sea Trout Fishing.

HARRIS, GRAEME &
MORGAN, MOC
Successful Sea Trout Angling,
Blandford, 1989.
An excellent guide to every
aspect of sea-trout fishing,
written by two leading experts.

HENZELL, H P
Fishing for Sea Trout, A&C
Black, 1949.

HOLIDAY, F W
River Fishing for Sea Trout,
Herbert Jenkins, 1960.
F W "Ted" Holiday lived in
Pembrokeshire and fished the
rivers Towy and Teifi.

LAMOND, HENRY
The Sea-Trout: a Study in Natural History, Sherratt & Hughes, 1916.

MOTTRAM, J C
Sea Trout and other Fishing Studies, The Field, 1923.

NALL, G H
The Life Of The Sea Trout, especially in Scottish Waters, with chapters on the reading & measuring of scales, Seeley Service, 1930.

PEEL, C V A
Wild Sports in the Outer Hebrides, Robinson, 1901.
Mostly shooting and natural history, but includes some sea-trout fishing.

STUART, HAMISH
The Book of the Sea Trout, Cape, 1917.

WALTHAM, JAMES
The Sea Trout and the Fly, Crowood, 2006.

SALMON FISHING

ASHLEY-COOPER, JOHN
The Great Salmon Rivers of Scotland, Witherby, 1980.
A useful guide to four great Scottish salmon rivers: Dee, Spey, Tay and Tweed.

BALFOUR-KINNEAR, G P R
Flying Salmon, Longmans, 1937.
Spinning Salmon, Longmans, 1937.

BULLER, FREDERICK
The Domesday Book of Giant Salmon: Volumes I & II, Constable, 2007 and 2010.
A magnificent work by one of the country's leading angling historians, recording details of the largest Atlantic salmon ever caught.

CHAYTOR, A H
Letters to a Salmon Fisher's Sons, Murray, 1910.
Charmingly written in the form of letters to the author's two sons, showing the love, enthusiasm, acute observations and knowledge of a great salmon fisherman. Its advice is as relevant today as it was on the day of its first publication.

"At every new reading, the fisherman will find himself learning something he had missed before." (Ransome).

CROSSLEY, ANTHONY
The Floating Line for Salmon and Sea Trout, Methuen, 1948. An "...extremely alert account of Wood's methods." (Ransome).

CROW, S H
Hampshire Avon Salmon, Angling Times, 1966. "Few people know the Hampshire Avon and its salmon fishing better than Lt. Col. S H Crow [who] has been bailiff to Lord Normanton on the Somerley Water for eleven years".

GAINES, CHARLES & BURKE, MONTE (EDITORS)
In Search of Silver, Duncan Baird, 2001. A delightful and beautifully illustrated anthology of salmon fishing worldwide.

GILBERT, H A
The Tale of a Wye Fisherman, 2nd edition, Cape, 1953. Although first published in 1929, it is the second edition that tells the story of Robert Pashley, "who has fished the Wye since 1906 and in one year, using for the most part a trout rod and small flies, killed 678 salmon." (Ransome).

FALKUS, HUGH
Salmon Fishing: A Practical Guide, Witherby, 1984. A classic work on salmon fishing from one of its leading exponents.

NICKSON, GEOFFREY
A Portrait of Salmon Fishing, Anthony Atha, 1976. A beautifully produced anthology, illustrated by the delightful paintings of Tim Havers.

OGLESBY, ARTHUR
Salmon, Macdonald, 1971. A very good introduction by one of the leading salmon anglers of his generation.

QUARRY, WILLIAM W
Salmon Fishing and the Story of the River Tweed, Medlar Press, 2015. A magnificent book on salmon fishing and on the UK's most productive salmon river.

SCOTT, JOCK
Greased Line Fishing for Salmon, compiled from the fishing papers of the late A H E Wood, of Glassel, Seeley Service, 1935.
Fine and Far Off, Seeley Service, 1952.
"Jock Scott" was the pen-name of Donald G Ferris Rudd, a prolific author on salmon fishing who promoted the original and highly successful methods of A H E Wood.

SCROPE, WILLIAM
Days and Nights of Salmon Fishing in the River Tweed, Murray, 1843,

SPENCER, SIDNEY
Salmon and Seatrout in Wild Places, Witherby, 1968.
Newly from the Sea, Witherby, 1969.
Irish and Hebridean flyfishing for salmon and sea-trout - on loch, sea and river.

SUTTERBY, RODERICK & GREENHALGH, MALCOLM
Atlantic Salmon: An Illustrated Natural History, Merlin Unwin, 2005.

TAVERNER, ERIC
Salmon Fishing, Seeley Service, 1931.
Another encyclopaedic volume in the Lonsdale Library series. For many years this was the bible of salmon fishing.

WADDINGTON, RICHARD
Salmon Fishing: A New Philosophy, Davies, 1947.
Fly Fishing for Salmon: a Modern Technique, Faber, 1951.
Salmon Fishing: Philosophy And Practice, Faber, 1959.
Catching Salmon, David & Charles, 1978.
Waddington On Salmon Fishing, Crowood, 1991.

WALMSLEY, SAMUEL
Salmon Fishing - A Red Letter Day on the Hodder, reprinted from the *Blackburn Times*, 1929.

WEBSTER, GARY
Spinning for Salmon, Robert Hale, 2010.

BLACKER, WILLIAM
The Art of Fly-Making,
published by the author, 1842.
Blacker set up as a fly-dresser
and tackle-dealer in Soho in the
1820's. His exciting salmon-fly
patterns were among the first
to use exotic materials, creating
the salmon fly as an art form,
seducing the fishermen as much
as the fish. His book was first
published in 1842, then re-
issued in 1855 with wonderful
new colour plates.

CLEGG, THOMAS
*Tube Flies and How to Make
Them,* Messeena, 1962.
Hair and Fur in Fly Dressing,
Tom Saville, 1962.
Modern Tube Fly Making, Tom
Saville, 1965.
The Truth About Fluorescents,
Tom Saville, 1967.

DEERY, PATSY
*Irish Mayflies: A Fly-Fisher's
Guide,* Ken Smith Publishing,
2007.

DUNNE, J W
Sunshine and the Dry Fly, A&C
Black, 1924.
Dunne was the inventor of trout
flies with translucent bodies. A
delightful and important book
on trout fishing.

EDMONDS, H H & LEE, N N
*Brook And River Trouting:
a manual of modern North
Country methods,* published by
the authors, 1916.

EDWARDS, OLIVER
*Oliver Edwards' Flytyers
Masterclass,* Merlin Unwin
Books, 1994.
Oliver Edwards is one of the
UK's leading imitative fly
dressers. Essential reading.

EVANS, EMRYS
*Plu Stiniog: Trout Flies for
North Wales,* Coch-y-Bonddu
Books, 2010.

GATHERCOLE, PETER
The Fly-Tying Bible, Aurum, 2003.
Fly-Tying for Beginners, Aurum,
2005.
The two best introductions to
the subject.

GODDARD, JOHN
Trout Fly Recognition, A&C
Black, 1966.
*John Goddard's Waterside
Guide: an angler's pocket
reference to the insects of rivers
and lakes, how to identify
them and choose the matching
artificial*, Unwin Hyman, 1988.
*The Trout Fly Patterns of John
Goddard*, Merlin Unwin Books,
2004.
John Goddard also co-authored,
with Brian Clarke, *The Trout
and the Fly: A Modern Approach*,
Benn, 1980, one of the most
important modern books on
flyfishing, publishing ground-
breaking material on rise-forms,
presentation, and on the way
natural and artificial flies appear
to the trout.

GREENHALGH, MALCOLM &
OVENDEN, DENYS
*The Complete Fly-Fisher's
Handbook: the natural foods
of trout and grayling and their
artificial imitations*,
Dorling Kindersley, 1998.

GREENHALGH, MALCOLM &
SMALLEY, JASON
An Encyclopedia of Fishing Flies,
Collins, 2009.
An essential reference to fishing-
flies from around the world.

GRIFFITHS, TERRY (EDITOR)
*The Essential Kelson: a Fly Tyer's
Compendium*,
Coch-y-Bonddu Books, 2011.
A stunning book on the salmon
flies of George Kelson, including
78 photographs of Kelson flies
dressed by master salmon fly-
dresser Marvin Nolte.

HALE, J H
How to Tie Salmon Flies,
Sampson Low & Co., 1892.

HALFORD, FREDERIC M
*Floating Flies and How to Dress
Them*, Sampson Low & Co.,
1886.
*Dry Fly Fishing in Theory and
Practice*, Sampson Low & Co.,
1889.
Dry Fly Entomology, Vinton,
1897.
*Modern Development of the Dry
Fly*, Routledge, 1910.
The Dry-Fly Man's Handbook,
Routledge, 1913.

HARD, SVEN-OLOV
Tied in the Hand: Odyssey of a Salmon Fly-tyer, Coch-y-Bonddu Books, 2012.
Another beautifully produced book on classic salmon flies, complete with images of fully-dressed flies tied by the author without the aid of a vice.

HARWOOD, J KEITH
The Hardy Book of the Salmon Fly, Medlar Press, 2006.
A short, useful guide to the development of the salmon fly, complete with patterns.

HARRIS, J R
An Angler's Entomology, Collins New Naturalist series, 1952.

HEADLEY, STAN
Trout and Salmon Flies of Scotland, Merlin Unwin Books, 1997.

JORGENSEN, POUL
Salmon Flies, Their Character, Style and Dressing, Stackpole Books, 1978.
One of the best guides to dressing the classic salmon fly.

Kelson, G M
The Salmon Fly, published by the author, 1895.

LEESON, TED & SCHOLLMEYER, JIM
The Fly Tier's Benchside Reference to Techniques and Dressing Styles, Frank Amato Publications, 1998.
One of the most comprehensive books on fly-tying techniques ever produced and illustrated in colour with excellent step-by-step photographs.

MCCLELLAND, H
How to Tie Flies for Trout and Grayling, Fishing Gazette, 1899.

MAGEE, LESLIE
Fly Fishing: The North Country Tradition, Smith Settle, 1994.

MALONE, E J
Irish Trout and Salmon Flies, Colin Smythe, 1984.
Tying Flies in the Irish Style, Smith Settle, 2000.
Two outstanding books on Irish flies.

MANN, CHRIS
The Complete Illustrated Dictionary of Salmon Flies, Merlin Unwin, 2008.
A very comprehensive guide to salmon fly patterns old and new.

MORGAN, MOC
Fly Patterns for the Rivers and Lakes of Wales, Gomer, 1984. Later updated as *Trout and Salmon Flies of Wales*, Merlin Unwin, 1996.

MOSELY, MARTIN
The Dry-Fly Fisherman's Entomology, Routledge, 1921. Martin Mosely was a noted entomologist and published many books and scientific papers on aquatic entomology.

MOTTRAM, J C
Fly-Fishing: Some New Arts and Mysteries, The Field, 1915.
"I had come to think of him as the completely unsung genius of English angling literature. I consider Some New Arts and Mysteries one of the most innovative fishing books ever written." (Arnold Gingrich).

O'REILLY, PAT
Matching the Hatch: Stillwater, River and Stream, Swan Hill, 1997.

O'REILLY, PETER
Trout and Salmon Flies of Ireland, Merlin Unwin, 1995.

PRITT, T E
Yorkshire Trout Flies, Goodall & Suddick, 1885.
Re-issued by Sampson Low & Co. in 1886 with the revised title, *North Country Flies*.
At the time, the definitive book on North Country soft-hackle wet flies and fishing.

PRYCE-TANNATT, T E
How to Dress Salmon Flies, Black, 1914.

RADENCICH, MICHAEL D
Tying the Classic Salmon Fly, Stackpole Books, 1997.
Classic Salmon Fly Materials, Stackpole Books, 2007.
Twenty Salmon Flies, Stackpole Books, 2010.
Classic Salmon Fly Patterns, Stackpole Books, 2012.
Indispensable for the fly-tyer who wants to dress classic salmon flies.

RANSOME, ARTHUR
Mainly About Fishing, A&C Black, 1959.
A must for anyone interested in the history of the salmon fly.

ROBERTS, JOHN
The New Illustrated Dictionary of Trout Flies, George, Allen & Unwin, 1986.
A Guide to River Trout Flies, Crowood, 1989.

ROBSON, KENNETH
Robson's Guide: Stillwater Trout Flies, an Alphabetical Survey in Colour, Beekay, 1985.

RONALDS, ALFRED
The Fly-Fisher's Entomology, Longmans, 1836.
Alfred Ronalds was the first of the great angler-naturalists. His book revolutionised flyfishing and fly-tying, and formed the cornerstone on which all later books on angling entomology were based.

SAWADA, KEN
The Art of the Classic Salmon Fly, Kodansha, 1989.
A truly magnificent book, bound in black velvet and slip-cased, containing stunning photographs of classic salmon flies. A bibliophile's delight.

SCHMOOKLER, PAUL & SILS, INGRID, V
Rare and Unusual Fly Tying Materials: A Natural History, Volume 1 Birds, published by the authors, 1994.
Volume 2 Birds and Mammals, published by the authors, 1997.
Two magnificent volumes for the serious fly-dresser.

SHARP, ROBERT
Let's Fish the Clyde, Motherwell Times, 1973.
A scarce and much sought-after treatise on the trout flies of the River Clyde in Scotland, and on the methods of tying and fishing them.

SMITH, ROBERT L
The North Country Fly: Yorkshire's Soft Hackle Tradition, Coch-y-Bonddu Books, 2015.
An authoritative history of north-country spider fishing and fly-tying.

SWARBRICK, JOHN
List of Wharfedale Flies, 1807, Hemsley, 1907.
Luckily there is a modern reprint available - as a collectable miniature book.

HARRY, VALLACK
Fishing Flies for Upper Teesdale,
published by the author, 2008.

VAN BORK, HENK
Salmon Flies: Past and Present,
Coch-y-Bonddu Books, 2014.
A beautifully produced and
illustrated book on the history
of salmon flies, complete with
step-by-step tying diagrams.

WAKEFORD, JACQUELINE
*Flytying Techniques: A Full
Colour Guide,* Benn, 1980.
One of the best 'how to' books
of the last fifty years.

WALTHAM, JAMES
Sea Trout Flies, A&C Black, 1988.

WATSON, JOHN N
*Angling with the Fly: flies
& anglers of Derbyshire and
Staffordshire,* Ken Smith, 2009.
*The Forgotten Flies of Roger
Woolley,* Coch-y-Bonddu Books,
2012.

WEST, LEONARD
*The Natural Trout Fly And Its
Imitation,* published by the
author, 1912.

WILLIAMS, A COURTNEY
A Dictionary of Trout Flies,
Black, 1949.
Still one of the best sources
of dressings, particularly for
traditional trout flies.

WOOLLEY, ROGER
Modern Trout Fly Dressing,
Fishing Gazette, 1932.
This well respected manual by
a well-respected professional
fly-dresser is based on sound
entomology. It is good on all
trout flies but especially strong
on regional and north country
soft-hackle patterns.

YOUNGER, JIMMY & GLORIA
*"The Book" : Salmon, Trout and
Sea-Trout Flies,*
published by the authors, 1997.

CHAPTER TEN

The Angler's Library III

Coarse and Sea Fishing Books

When Arthur Ransome published *Fishing* in 1955 he listed just seven titles under the heading *Coarse Fishing*, although his list did include the recently published *Still-Water Angling* by Richard Walker (1952). It was Dick Walker, together with the likes of Fred J. Taylor, Peter Stone and Fred Buller, to name but a few, who revolutionised coarse fishing during the 1950s and 1960s. They taught that big fish could be caught by design rather than by accident and heralded in the era of specimen angling. The fifty or so years since then have witnessed a revolution in our approach to coarse fishing, not only in the development of new methods and techniques but also in the development of tackle and the growth of commercial fisheries, where anglers can almost be guaranteed fish of a size undreamed of before.

This tremendous growth in coarse fishing has led to a plethora of books devoted to the subject, especially in the monographs on particular species. It has been a difficult task surveying such a wide field of literature and I have tried to keep to Ransome's principles by sub-dividing the books into different categories and listing them in alphabetical order. Again, I am very aware that such a list is subjective and is based largely on my own collecting habits over the last thirty years. The popularity of coarse fishing and the demand for books on the subject has led to a large increase in the price of some of the classic titles of this period in the second-hand book market.

It appears that Ransome was not a particularly keen sea angler and in his bibliography he failed to include any books on this branch of the sport. This omission has now been rectified and a list of popular sea angling books has been added.

PIKE AND PREDATOR FISHING

BAILEY, JOHN & MILLER, ROGER
Perch: Contemporary Days and Ways, Crowood, 1989.

BARRETT, MARK
Zander Fishing: A Complete Guide, Crowood, 2008.

BETTELL, CHARLIE
The Art of Lure Fishing, Crowood, 1994.
A useful guide to a rapidly growing branch of angling.

BOOTH, GRAHAM
A History of Pike Fishing: Volumes I and II, Harper, 2011 & 2015.
Two beautifully produced volumes that together form a comprehensive history of pike fishing. Essential reading for the serious pike angler and angling historian.

BULLER, FRED
Pike, Macdonald, 1971. Later republished as *Pike and the Pike Angler*, Stanley Paul, 1981.
The Domesday Book of Mammoth Pike, Stanley Paul, 1979.
More Mammoth Pike, Medlar Press, 2005.

CHOLMONDELEY-PENNELL, H
The Book of the Pike, Hardwicke, 1865.

GUSTAFSON, PAUL
How to Catch Bigger Pike, Collins Willow, 1997.

HOLGATE, JAMES
Reflections Upon Lakeland Angling, published by the author, 1989.
James Holgate (1957-2009) was a prolific writer on pike fishing matters, and editor of *Pike and Predators* magazine.

MARTIN, J W
Pike and Perch Fishing, The Angler, 1898.
A new edition, retitled *Days Among the Pike and Perch*, published for the author, 1907.

MORGAN, PAUL
The Pike Angler's Library, Coch-y-Bonddu Books, 1998.
A fine bibliography of the pike by the well-known bibliopolist.

PAGE, MARTYN & BELLARS, VIC
Pike: In Pursuit of Esox Lucius, Crowood, 1990.
A very comprehensive study of pike fishing by two of its leading exponents.

PERCHFISHERS, THE
The Book of the Perch, edited by Peter Rogers & Steve Burke, Oxford Illustrated Press, 1990.
The Biggest Fish of All, edited by John McAngus, Tony Meers, Richard Chandaman & Mick Stevens, Harper, 2011.

PUGH, DAVE
Lure Fishing: Presentation & Strategy, Coch-y-Bonddu Books, 2014.
The author, a specialist in the slow and coloured waters of the lower Severn, explains his methods, principally for pike and zander.

RICKARDS, BARRIE
Big Pike, A&C Black, 1986.

RICKARDS, BARRIE & BANNISTER, MALCOLM
The Ten Greatest Pike Anglers, Boydell Press, 1991.
The Great Modern Pike Anglers, Crowood, 2006.

RICKARDS, BARRIE & FICKLING, NEVILLE, J
Zander, A&C Black, 1979.
A comprehensive book by two of our leading predator anglers.

ROGOWSKI, STEVE
Pike Fishing in the UK and Ireland, Crowood, 2006.
An excellent guide to the leading pike venues.

SIDLEY, JOHN
River Piking, Boydell, 1987.

WATSON, JOHN
A Piker's Progress, Creel, 1991.
Later updated as *A Piker's Progression*, Creel, 2010.
Two highly readable books from the pen of one of the country's leading pike anglers.

CARP FISHING

CLIFFORD, KEVIN
A History of Carp Fishing,
Sandholme Publishing, 1992
A fascinating and well-
researched book on the history
of carp angling.

CLIFFORD, KEVIN & ARBERY,
LEN
Redmire Pool, Beekay, 1984.
Redmire Pool on the Welsh
borders is where Richard
Walker and Chris Yates caught
their legendary record breaking
carp.

GIBBINSON, JIM
Carp, MacDonald, 1968.
One of the earlier and highly
regarded monographs on carp
fishing.

HUTCHINSON, ROD
The Carp Strikes Back,
Wonderdog Publications, 1983.
One of the pioneers of modern
carp fishing reveals his methods
and tactics. All Rod's books are
worthy of a place on the carp
angler's bookshelves.

INGHAM, MAURICE &
WALKER, RICHARD
*Drop Me a Line: being letters
exchanged on trout and coarse
fishing*, MacGibbon & Kee,
1953.
An exchange of letters between
Richard Walker and Maurice
Ingham, primarily concerning
carp fishing.

INGHAM MAURICE &
ROGERS, PETER
The Carp Catchers' Club, Medlar
Press, 1998.
A fascinating compilation of
letters between Ingham, Walker,
Venables and other members
of the famous Carp Catchers'
Club.

LANGRIDGE, JOHN
Aphrodite's Carp, Medlar Press,
2007.
A complete history of Britain's
favourite fish.

MADDOCKS, KEVIN
Carp Fever, Beekay, 1981.
One of the great carp anglers
shares his methods, tactics and
memorable catches.

MOHAN, PETER
Cypry, the Story of a Carp,
Pelham, 1973.
A look at the world through the
eyes of a carp.

ROLFE, PETER
*Crock of Gold: Seeking the
Crucian Carp*, MPress, 2010.

WATKINS-PITCHFORD, DENYS
*Confessions of a Carp Fisher, by
"BB,"* Eyre & Spottiswoode, 1950.
*A Carp Water: Wood Pool, by
"BB,"* Putnam, 1958.

YATES, CHRISTOPHER
Casting at the Sun, Pelham,
1986.
The Secret Carp, Merlin Unwin,
1992.
*Four Seasons: Fishing Diaries
1977-1981*, Medlar Press, 1996.
The Lost Diary, Unbound, 2013.
Chris Yates, one of our greatest
living angling writers, recounts
his carp fishing adventures

BARBEL FISHING

BARBEL CATCHERS &
FRIENDS
Barbel, Crowood, 1988.
Revised and updated as *Barbel
Rivers and Captures* , Crowood,
2004.
A comprehensive survey
of barbel rivers and fishing
methods.

BERRY, JON
A Can Of Worms: *the story of
barbel and the men who fished
for them*, Medlar Press, 2007.

CROUCH, FRED
Understanding Barbel, Pelham
Books, 1986.
An in-depth study of the barbel
from one of the country's
greatest barbel anglers.

MILES, TONY
Elite Barbel, Little Egret Press,
2004.

MILES, TONY & WEST, TREFOR
Quest For Barbel, Crowood, 1991.
Two leading barbel anglers give
a detailed insight into their
fishing methods.

ORME, ANDY
Barbel Mania, Crowood, 1990.
A very good introduction to
barbel biology and fishing
methods, written by an angler
who is also a freshwater
biologist.

STONE, PETER
Bream and Barbel, Angling
Times, 1963.
A highly collectable book
from an author who needs no
introduction.

WHEAT, PETER
The Fighting Barbel, Ernest
Benn, 1967.
One of the classic works on
barbel fishing.

GENERAL COARSE ANGLING BOOKS:
Books on bream, chub, dace, eels, roach, tench, or on a variety
of species

ARBERY, LEN
In Pursuit of Big Tench,
Crowood, 1996.

BAILEY, JOHN
In Visible Waters, Crowood, 1984.
Roach: The Gentle Giants,
Crowood, 1987.
*The Fishing Detective: A New
Approach to Coarse Angling*,
Collins, 1994.

BAILEY, JOHN & MILLER,
ROGER
Bream: Tales and Tactics,
Crowood, 1988.

CHOLMONDELEY-PENNELL, H
*Fishing: Pike and Other Coarse
Fish*, The Badminton Library,
Longmans, Green & Co., 1885.
The standard work on coarse
fishing at the end of the 19th
century.

CHUB STUDY GROUP
*Chub: Commemorating Twenty-
One Years Of The Chub Study
Group*, edited by Graham
Cornish & Len Cacutt, The
Chub Study Group, 1994.

CLIFFORD, W G
Holiday Angling (Mainly for Roach), Bles, 1925.

EVERARD, MARK
Dace: The Prince of the Stream, MPress, 2011.
The Complete Book of the Roach, Medlar Press, 2006.
Redfin Diaries, Coch-y-Bonddu Books, 2013.

FENNELL, GREVILLE
The Book of the Roach, Sampson Low & Co., 1870.
The earliest coarse fishing monograph and one of the very few books devoted solely to roach fishing.

FORT, TOM
The Book of Eels, Harper Collins, 2002.
This is not a 'how to' book but a fascinating glimpse into the mysterious world of the eel. An excellent read.

GARNETT, DOMINIC
Flyfishing for Coarse Fish, Merlin Unwin, 2012.
Canal Fishing, Merlin Unwin, 2014.

HOOPER, MARTIN
Specimen Angling By Design, Crowood, 1993.

LANE, BILLY & GRAHAM, COLIN
Billy Lane's Encyclopaedia of Float Fishing, Pelham, 1971.
A superb guide to float fishing by a true master of the art.

McCONNELL, BARRY
The Eel Angler, Harper, 2012.
A beautifully produced book covering all aspects of fishing for eels.

MANSFIELD, KENNETH
The How To Catch Them Series, Herbert Jenkins, 1954-1969.
Mansfield edited this popular series of 44 pocket-sized monographs on different quarry species, and the methods used to catch them. Individual experts contributed volumes on most species of coarse fish, as well as some on sea and game fish.

MARTIN, J W
Float Fishing and Spinning in the Nottingham Style, Sampson Low, 1882.
The Trent Otter's Little Book on Angling, Simpkin, 1910.
Coarse Fish Angling, Cape, 1924
J W Martin was a well-known fishing tackle dealer and wrote under the pen-name "The Trent Otter."

MILES, TONY
My Way With Chub, Ironbridge Publications, 1988.
Search For Big Chub, Crowood, 1996.

PARKER, ERIC
Fine Angling for Coarse Fish, Seeley Service, 1930.
The standard handbook for coarse anglers through much of the twentieth century. Yet another encyclopaedic volume in the Lonsdale Library series.

PARKER, L A
This Fishing, Bennett Brothers, 1948.
Captain Parker was landlord of The Bull at Downton, on the Hampshire Avon, and a great authority on roach fishing. Chapters on hemp fishing, long-trotting, pole fishing, the Avon and the Arun, trout and pike, carp and barbel fishing.

ROGERS, PETER (EDITOR)
Red Letter Days, Crowood, 1994.
This book is a tribute to Bernard Venables. It contains forty-eight golden memories from some of our greatest angling writers and is beautifully illustrated by John Searl.

SEAMAN, KENNETH
The Complete Chub Angler, David and Charles, 1976.
Looks at the natural history of the chub and covers the main chub fishing techniques.

SEARL, JOHN
Chalk Stream Roach: The Ultimate Challenge, privately published, 2009.
The chalkstreams are not just the home of large trout, they also contain specimen roach and this volume, illustrated by the author, explores how they can be caught.

SHERINGHAM H T
Coarse Fishing, A&C Black, 1912.
One of the classic handbooks

on all kinds of coarse angling
- interspersed with good
anecdotes.

SIDLEY, JOHN
Eels, Beekay, 1990.
A comprehensive guide to eel
fishing.

TAYLOR, FRED J
Angling in Earnest, MacGibbon
and Kee, 1958.
*Favourite Swims and Still Water
Pitches*, MacGibbon and Kee,
1961.
Tench, Macdonald, 1971.

TURNBULL, CHRIS
A Time for Tench, published by
the author, 2004.
*Reflections: Highlights from an
Angling Life*, Harper, 2011.
Beautifully illustrated books by
an expert artist-angler.

WALKER, RICHARD
Rod Building for Amateurs,
Belfield & Bushell, 1952.
Still Water Angling, Macgibbon
& Kee, 1953.
How Fish Feed, Angling Times,
1959.
*Catching Fish: Knowing their
feeding habits*, David and
Charles, 1981.

WALSINGHAM, MARK
A Fool and his Eel, Freebird,
2012.

WILSON, JOHN
*John Wilson's Coarse Fishing
Method Manual*, Boxtree, 1997.
An indispensable guide,
beautifully illustrated, to
modern coarse fishing methods.

YATES, CHRISTOPHER
How to Fish, Hamish Hamilton,
2006.
This not really a 'how to'
book at all, but a collection of
bankside jottings by one of our
greatest living angling writers.
Anything by Yates is a must for
the angler's library.

DARLING, JOHN
Bass Fishing on Shore and Sea,
Crowood, 1996.

GAMMON, CLIVE
A Tide of Fish, Heinemann, 1962.
The classic of South Wales bass
and tope fishing.

GARRAD J P
*Sea Angling with the Baited
Spoon*, by "Seangler," Herbert
Jenkins, 1960.
This is one of the most detailed
studies of any fishing method, and
was entirely innovative in its day.
An important monograph on a
little-studied aspect of sea angling.

GREEN, LINDSEY
The Challenge of Sea Fishing,
published by the author, 2013.

KENNEDY, MICHAEL
The Sea Angler's Fishes,
Hutchinson, 1954.

LADLE, MIKE WITH HARRY
CASEY & TERRY GLEDHILL.
Operation Sea Angler, A&C
Black, 1983.
One of the most innovative
modern books on sea angling,
with excellent (and, at the time
of publication, ground-breaking)
chapters on plug-fishing for bass
and flyfishing for mullet.

LADLE, MIKE & VAUGHAN,
ALAN
Hooked on Bass, Crowood, 1988.

MITCHELL-HEDGES, F A
Battles with Giant Fish,
Duckworth, 1923.
Big-game fishing adventures in
Central America.

Morgan, Paul (editor)
*Saltwater Flyfishing: Britain &
Northern Europe*,
Coch-y-Bonddu Books, 1998.

PEARSON, ANTHONY
Successful Shore Fishing,
Newnes, 1967.
An evocative account of surf-
fishing in Wales and Ireland in
the 1960's. Mostly about bass
fishing, but includes chapters on
Lancashire and Yorkshire cod.

ROSS, MARK
*The Glory Days of the Giant
Scarborough Tunny: The British
Tunny Club, Hardy Bros tackle*

and big game fishing in the 1930s, published by the author, 2010

SMITH, SIMON
Running with the Tide, Medlar Press, 2013.

STOKER, HUGH (EDITOR)
Sea Angling with the Specimen Hunters, Benn, 1977.
This is one very useful example of Hugh Stoker's prolific output on sea angling.

THRUSSELL, MIKE
Addicted to Angling: A Lifetime's Obsession with Fish and Fishing, Peridot Press, 2015.
An excellent account of one man's passion for sea fishing.

YATES, CHRIS
Out of the Blue: On Fishing at Sea, Hamilton, 2003.

Editor's note to the book lists

In most instances we have only listed the date of first publication. Many of these books were reprinted or went into several editions, and some have modern facsimiles. The Flyfisher's Classic Library specialise in producing high-quality editions of the most important flyfishing books, and many of these are currently in print (including Ransome's *The Fisherman's Library*). Other publishers such as the Medlar Press, Little Egret Press and Coch-y-Bonddu Books have also made available important angling books that had previously been out-of-print.

The primary source for second-hand or antiquarian angling books used to be specialist bookseller's catalogues. The digital age has seen the demise of the traditional hard-copy catalogue (*pace* Callahan & Company of Peterborough, New Hampshire), but an increase in the availability of information about books on websites such as Abebooks and Amazon. There are still specialists such as Hereward Books and Coch-y-Bonddu Books, and these also list on the internet. However it is worth bearing in mind that their stocks far exceed their internet listings and that a call to their premises is more likely to turn up the unusual items. Other sources of out-of-print books are discussed by the author in Chapter One, *The Angling Bibliophile.*

'DESERT ISLAND' BOOKS

If I were stranded on a desert island I would like to have the following ten books with me.

Angling and Art in Scotland
Ernest E Briggs, Longmans, Green, and Co., 1908.

This book combines two of my major interests, angling and art. The author was a very accomplished watercolour artist and this volume is illustrated with his beautiful watercolours and black and white illustrations. It is a book of two halves. In the first half the author describes his fishing experiences in Galloway, one of my favourite parts of Scotland where I have spent many happy holidays. In the second half the author relates his fishing experiences in the Highlands in many of the areas where I have also fished. The late Ron Coleby, bibliopolist and bibliophile, thought that this book 'must approach the ideal angling book,' and I agree with him.

Once A Flyfisher
Laurence Catlow, Merlin Unwin Books, 2001.

Before his retirement, Laurence Catlow taught classics at Sedbergh School in Cumbria and in his spare time he regularly fished the Wharfe and the Eden. This book, in the form of a diary, follows the events of a season on these rivers. It is beautifully written and transports me to the rivers where I have wet many a line.

The Deepening Pool
Chris Yates, Unwin Hyman, 1990.

Chris Yates is undoubtedly one of our most celebrated angling writers, best known, perhaps, for his capture of a 51 lb carp from Redmire Pool. This book, however, is not about carp but about barbel, and the author's rediscovery of the delights of river fishing, primarily on the Hampshire Avon. It is beautifully illustrated with Yates' evocative photographs. As a barbel angler myself, I feel I can relate to this book.

Trout Bum
John Gierach, Robinson Publishing (1st UK edition), 1993.

John Gierach does for American trout fishing what Chris Yates does for coarse fishing in this country. Both authors love to use bamboo rods and while Yates is a lover of tea, Gierach prefers his coffee fix.

Images of Angling
David Beazley, Creel Press, 2010.

This magnificently produced volume surveys three centuries of angling prints. It is not a book to read from cover to cover but a book to dip into and ponder over the beautiful illustrations contained within. It would transport the viewer away from the confines of a desert island.

Fishing in Wild Places
David Street, Golden Grove, 1989.

Like Street, I enjoy fishing in wild places and my quest for salmon and trout has led me from Shetland to Alaska. This book transports the reader to some of these wild and remote places and is beautifully written. Terence Lambert's evocative pencil illustrations enhance the quality of the writing.

Casting a Line
Malcolm Greenhalgh, Medlar Press, 2014.

I have known Malcolm, a member of my fishing club, for a good many years. He is a great raconteur and this autobiographical book abounds with amusing stories of his angling experiences both at home and abroad and includes many of the waters where I fish. This book would be a strong reminder of home.

Rod and Line
Arthur Ransome, Jonathan Cape, 1929.
I am a great admirer of the writings of Arthur Ransome. This volume contains a selection of articles that he wrote originally for his angling column in the *Guardian* newspaper. Ransome was a true all-round angler who was equally at home on a Hampshire chalk stream or Lakeland tarn.

One for the Road
Donald MacIntosh, Medlar Press, 2006.
This must surely be one of the funniest angling books ever written and would stop me from getting too depressed on a desert island. I laugh out loud every time I read these stories, which originally appeared in *Waterlog* magazine.

Oppian, Colluthus, Tryphiodorus
A W Mair (translator), Loeb Classical Library, Heinemann, 1963.
This may seem a very odd choice for a desert island book. Oppian, who lived in the 2nd century AD, wrote the *Halieutica*, the first fishing book to survive in western literature. As a former classics teacher, I would like to get to grips with this book and the parallel Greek and English text would help to keep my Ancient Greek up to scratch.

Authors listed in the Angler's Library